WRITER'S BLOCK

A Place to Hammer It Out, Set Your Creativity Free & Hone Your Craft

CAROL KILLMAN ROSENBERG

Disclaimer: This is a book of writing advice and activities, some requiring physical effort, intended to remotivate the reader to write. The content is based on the author's professional and personal experience and research. This book is not a substitute for professional mental-health advice, diagnosis, or treatment. The author and publisher encourage the reader to seek the advice of a qualified health professional with any questions the reader may have regarding a physical or mental health condition and/or the appropriateness of physical activity.

Published by
The Book Couple

The
BOOK
Couple
BOCA RATON, FL

BOCA RATON, FLORIDA
www.thebookcouple.com

Copyright © 2022 Carol Killman Rosenberg

ISBN-13: 978-1-7331571-1-7

Production by Gary A. Rosenberg

Fair Warning: Use a pen or pencil in this book. Markers will bleed through the page, but you already knew that, right? Use crayons or colored pencils to draw or color.

"Soon I'll find the right words,
they'll be very simple."
~Jack Kerouac

You will find the right words, too.

Whether or not they're simple is up to you.

writer's block. noun : an obstacle in the mind that prevents a writer from starting or moving forward with piece of writing, such as a book, play, poem, article, letter, or catchy social media post.

Stumped for your next idea—or word?

You've come to the *write* place. Here's where you can work that "mind obstacle" out of your head by pounding the pages of this book with your pen or pencil. You can also toss it aside when prompted and go find inspiration elsewhere or just give yourself a much-needed mental break to get your creativity flowing again.

With this book, there's no cursor flashing at you, blink-blink-blinking, waiting for your fingers to fly across the keyboard. Write or scribble all over the pages. Respond to the activity prompts (some will get you out of your chair!) or don't. Flip to a random page and see if it calls to you. If not, flip again or check out the handy guide on page 290.

This is your Writer's Block and yours alone. Stash your book in a safe place and break it out whenever your inner muse takes an impromptu day off—or maybe even an extended vacation. You will be amazed by the awesomeness that comes out of your head when you give your mind some wiggle room to get around the block standing between you and the written page.

Starting Now...

See those blank lines over there? Use them to write down *exactly* what you're thinking at this moment.

Your mind's not blank. You've got stuff going on in there for sure. Even if it's your to-do list, put your pen to the page. If you're stuck on thoughts about the future or the past, or if something else is taking up space in your head—Get. It. Out.

You can be completely honest. No one's looking over your shoulder, apparently not even your muse. But that's okay—you're good with that *for now*. It's why you're here.

"Start writing, no matter what. The water does not flow until the faucet is turned on." ~Louis L'Amour

What's Causing Your Block?

Writing difficulties can occur for any number of reasons. Getting to know your variety of Writer's Block on any given day can help you come up with strategies to get around the obstacle or, even better, smash it to pieces.

Check off all the scenarios that describe your situation. It might be different each time you visit this book. Whatever it is, you can be sure there's an activity here that will renew your motivation and set your creativity free.

- ☐ You strive for perfection.
- ☐ You lack interest in your topic.
- ☐ You were tossing and turning all night.
- ☐ Inspiration is in short supply.
- ☐ Your eyes need to look at something other than a screen.
- ☐ Life is stressing you out.
- ☐ You're stuck in the details.
- ☐ You're missing the details.
- ☐ Your perspective is too narrow.
- ☐ You feel like a slow-moving sloth.
- ☐ Your mind is going too fast.
- ☐ The coffee pot is empty.
- ☐ Your emotions are off the charts.

- ☐ You fear failure (and who doesn't?).
- ☐ Someone is pressuring you to write.
- ☐ *You* are the someone pressuring you to write.
- ☐ You aren't connecting to your work.
- ☐ You're just not in the mood to write.
- ☐ All the "rules" are freaking you out.
- ☐ You fear rejection and/or criticism.
- ☐ You're questioning your ability to write well.
- ☐ You don't have a place to write.
- ☐ The distractions around you are driving you to, well, distraction.
- ☐ You have a headache.
- ☐ Your writing habits are unstructured.
- ☐ Your writing habits are *too* structured.
- ☐ You're afraid of your readers.
- ☐ You have so many other things you need to do.
- ☐ Other _____
- ☐ Other _____
- ☐ Other _____

Not sure where to start? There's a handy guide on page 290.

To Write or Not to Write?

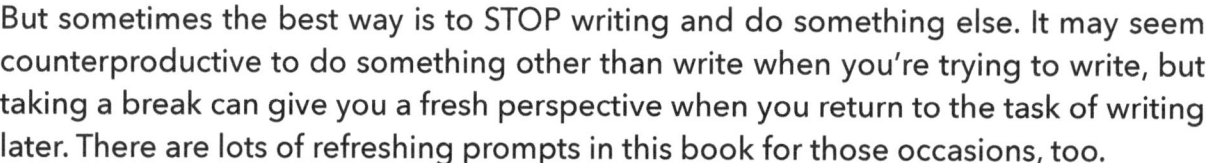

That's today's question. Sometimes the best way to break through your Writer's Block is to just keep writing—anything. You'll find lots of writing prompts in these pages to feed your creativity and get that mental muscle moving.

But sometimes the best way is to STOP writing and do something else. It may seem counterproductive to do something other than write when you're trying to write, but taking a break can give you a fresh perspective when you return to the task of writing later. There are lots of refreshing prompts in this book for those occasions, too.

Only you can figure out what you need at any given time. The idea is to find a balance. Obviously, you want to feel renewed motivation to continue writing, so avoiding the task entirely by filling your days and nights with distractions swings you too far to one side. On the other hand, forcing yourself to write when it's getting you nowhere (even if all the advice is to "write, write, write") is too far to the other side.

How to find balance?

- ✓ If you have a deadline, you can't avoid writing for too long. Schedule short breaks to do something other than write between your daily writing sessions.

- ✓ If you have a self-imposed deadline, give yourself a day off to recharge, and then tackle your writing to-do list the next day.

- ✓ If it's been a long time since you've written anything, it's time to write something—anything—to get your creativity flowing again.

- ✓ If you've just completed a lengthy first draft, give yourself a break. Don't expect to tackle rewrites immediately upon completion with 100% brainpower. Take time to recoup your energy and celebrate making that first draft happen.

- ✓ Want to start something new, but you're fresh out of ideas? Spend time seeking inspiration elsewhere rather than trying to find it on a blank page.

- ✓ Schedule in "writing vacations" to reward yourself for a job well done. Let's say you've completed your manuscript and now it's with your editor. Have a staycation away from your writer's nook and computer or go somewhere you can relax.

These are just a few ways to find balance. Mix it up. Write one day; don't write the next. Whatever you do, don't let too much time pass between your writing days, even if on some of those days you just produce gibberish. There's plenty of room for that in this book!

"Never give up, for that is just the place and time that the tide will turn." ~Harriet Beecher Stowe

Imagine That . . .

Imagine that your Writer's Block is a character who is taking up space in your brain. You don't have to write this down if you don't want to. Just imagine. Giving your Writer's Block some personal characteristics can help you get to know it better. They say knowing is half the battle, so knowing your Writer's Block more intimately puts you halfway toward conquering it! Some examples are included here, but don't let that stop you from using your imagination.

- What does it say? *("Ha, ha, I've got you just where I want you!")*
- What's the quality of its voice? *(Like nails on a chalkboard? Loud? Soft? Cloyingly sweet?)*
- Is it male, female, neither, both? *(Single-cell slime mold?)*
- Does it have a name? *(Bob? Tina? Cricket?)*
- What is its most unusual feature? *(Slippery? Spiny? Big teeth?)*
- What makes it happy? *(A blank page? A flashing cursor?)*
- What brings it down? *(Elegant prose?)*
- What is its superpower? *(Keeping you from writing?)*
- What is its kryptonite? *(This book?)*
- What does it want most in its hopefully short life? *(To keep your creative juices from leaking out?)*
- What can you say to it to make it go away. *("Beat it, bud!")*

Picture This . . .

If your Writer's Block had color, texture, and shape (no, it doesn't *have* to be square), what would it look like? Visualize an image and draw what you see. Then grab some scrap paper, cut out a square, and paste the square over your drawing. *Poof!* It's gone.

"Writing about a writer's block is better than not writing at all." ~Charles Bukowski

(So is drawing it.)

Got Muse?

If not, here's a muse to use. Keep her near your writing pad or computer and see what happens. Hey, you never know.

"I learned to produce whether I wanted to or not. It would be easy to say oh, I have writer's block, oh, I have to wait for my muse. I don't. Chain that muse to your desk and get the job done." ~Barbara Kingsolver

Inspiration Is . . . Making You Wait

What usually inspires you? Is it:

- Sunshine on your shoulder? (It made John Denver happy.)
- A never-ending field of sunflowers?
- Waves crashing on the shore?
- A cup of cocoa on a cold winter's night?
- A passionate speech on an impactful topic?
- A moving piece of music?
- Stunning artwork?
- Children playing?
- People being kind to each other?

On the facing page, write down 10 things that normally inspire you. When you're all done, circle one or two of them you can go and experience right now. Stash this book away and seek out your inspiration. (You can even leave the club at home.)

Top-10 Sources of Inspiration

1. _____
2. _____
3. _____
4. _____
5. _____
6. _____
7. _____
8. _____
9. _____
10. _____

"Don't loaf and invite inspiration;
light out after it with a club."
~Jack London

A Dry Well of Inspiration

Is your usual source of inspiration not motivating you? Do the opposite. For instance, if you're usually inspired by:

- sunshine on your shoulder, take a walk on a rainy day without an umbrella.
- a never-ending field of sunflowers, contemplate a bowl of sunflower seeds.
- waves crashing on the shore, view images of the desert (or visit one).
- a cup of cocoa on a cold winter's night, have a glass of iced tea.
- a passionate speech on an impactful topic, watch a goofy comedian.
- a moving piece of music, listen to a song you can't stand.
- stunning artwork, scroll through pictures of "cake failures" on Google.
- children playing, watch an MMA fight.
- people being kind to each other, replay a presidential debate.

You just might find that seeking inspiration in places you wouldn't think of as inspiring may give you a fresh perspective.

Remember Your Writing "Whys"

Have you lost sight of why you became a writer in the first place? Has the task begun to feel aimless? It's time to remember your why. Check all that apply. Do you write to:

- ☐ Entertain others?
- ☐ Entertain yourself?
- ☐ Express yourself?
- ☐ Follow a calling?
- ☐ Change lives?
- ☐ Teach others?
- ☐ Make others think?
- ☐ Reach people?
- ☐ Make a difference?
- ☐ Leave a legacy?
- ☐ Enjoy the creative process?
- ☐ Feel fulfilled?
- ☐ Make money?
- ☐ Something else? _____

Once you've remembered the reasons you want to write in the first place, ask yourself, "What am I willing to do to make it happen?" Hopefully, your answer will include "sit down and write." But that's the problem, right? Turn the page.

What Needs to Happen?

Chances are there's more than one reason you aren't able to express yourself right now. So what needs to happen for your writing to happen? Review the following list, and if one or more of these "needs" isn't being met, check it off and then make it happen. None of these require you to actually write yet, so no pressure!

Do you need to:

- ☐ Schedule writing sessions for the time you have available?
- ☐ Seek inspiration?
- ☐ Tap into your creativity?
- ☐ Get a laptop that won't freeze in the middle of a document?
- ☐ Set up a writer's nook?
- ☐ Say no to some social engagements?
- ☐ Stop obsessively playing that game on your smartphone?

- ☐ Do more research?
- ☐ Get some rest?
- ☐ Set realistic goals?
- ☐ Turn off social media?
- ☐ Gain a fresh perspective?
- ☐ Sign up for a writing course?
- ☐ Make a commitment to yourself?
- ☐ Take a break from binge-watching?
- ☐ Find a place where you can be alone?
- ☐ Stop comparing yourself to bestselling authors?
- ☐ Read a book about writing to get your wheels turning?
- ☐ Take care of another important task that's been looming over you?

Whatever is keeping you from writing may simply be an excuse to not write, so if you can eliminate the excuses by meeting any needs you think are missing, you'll have a better idea of why you are having such difficulty. This can bring you a step closer to writing for real.

Write Just for Fun

You're stuck. Nothing is coming to you. This is NO FUN AT ALL! Close the document or shut the notebook, and give yourself some room to write just for the heck of it. Not sure what you'd write about? Consider one of these topics:

- A zombie apocalypse that breaks out on Halloween night at the house next door.
- A quick trip to the grocery store for a hard-to-find item during a record-breaking storm.
- Pet sitting for a great Dane with zero manners.
- Getting lost in the woods just as the sun is about to set and all you have with you is a can of tuna, two matches, and a pocket guide to the great outdoors.
- Suddenly realizing you've got a crush on your single next-door neighbor (assuming you're single, too).
- A fight scene between a butterfly and a wasp.
- A treasure hunt in the swamp on a hot summer day.
- Running into an old friend who has undergone a drastic transformation.

Give yourself a target word count. Keep it short. You don't have to make this another one of your writing to-dos. But if you find you've got more to say than the target you set for yourself, great! See how far this idea takes you.

"You can't think yourself out of a writing block; you have to write yourself out of a thinking block." ~John Rogers

Bedeviled by the [Details]

Sometimes you'll trip over words or run smack into an inspiration wall. Or maybe you're not confident writing a particular something, like a fight scene or a setting description or a romantic interlude.

Let me introduce you to your new best friend, the [BRACKETS] method.

Just slap a descriptor of the thing you're stuck on in brackets and move on. It can be specific, like [a big, dark room, hearth dominating one wall, full of low-burning coals], or it can be simple, like [idiocy ensues]. Even [SETTING] or [WORD] or [MORE HERE] will work.

When you're ready to go back and fix it, you can search for the bracket characters in your word-processing program.

"For now, just get the words out. Get the story down however you can get it down, then fix it." ~Neil Gaiman

Have an Opposite Day

Sometimes you need to turn things upside down to shake out the sediment that's settled on the bottom—like orange juice with pulp.

- If you usually feel most creative first thing in the morning, see what a late night inspires in you.
- If you usually write fiction, take a crack at nonfiction—or vice versa.
- Choose a different mug to sip from while you write.
- Type with two fingers.
- Write the ending first.
- Use an antonym for every adjective you're about to use.
- Wear your pajamas all day (or actually get dressed if PJs are your norm).
- Put on formal wear before sitting down to write.
- Take your laptop into your bed and stay there all day (with snacks and water in reach).
- Write longhand if you usually type, or type if you usually write longhand.

Gather Your Props

In theatrical productions, there's usually a props table in the wings where actors leave their essential props so they don't get lost between scenes. Are there specific but relatively small elements you want to make sure to incorporate into your work? Are there things you've seen that you feel would make a good prop in your next piece?

Maybe there's a prop one of your characters will use (think Frodo's ring or Cinderella's slipper) that you want to be sure is accounted for by the end, or perhaps there's a color scheme you want to weave into your work.

On the facing page, write down all those elements you think will bring subtle but important value to your work. Don't worry if you have to cross out or erase "props" as your work evolves or add others you want to go back and add. Check your "props table" from time to time, and make sure that anything you've included is neatly woven through the text and is accounted for at the end.

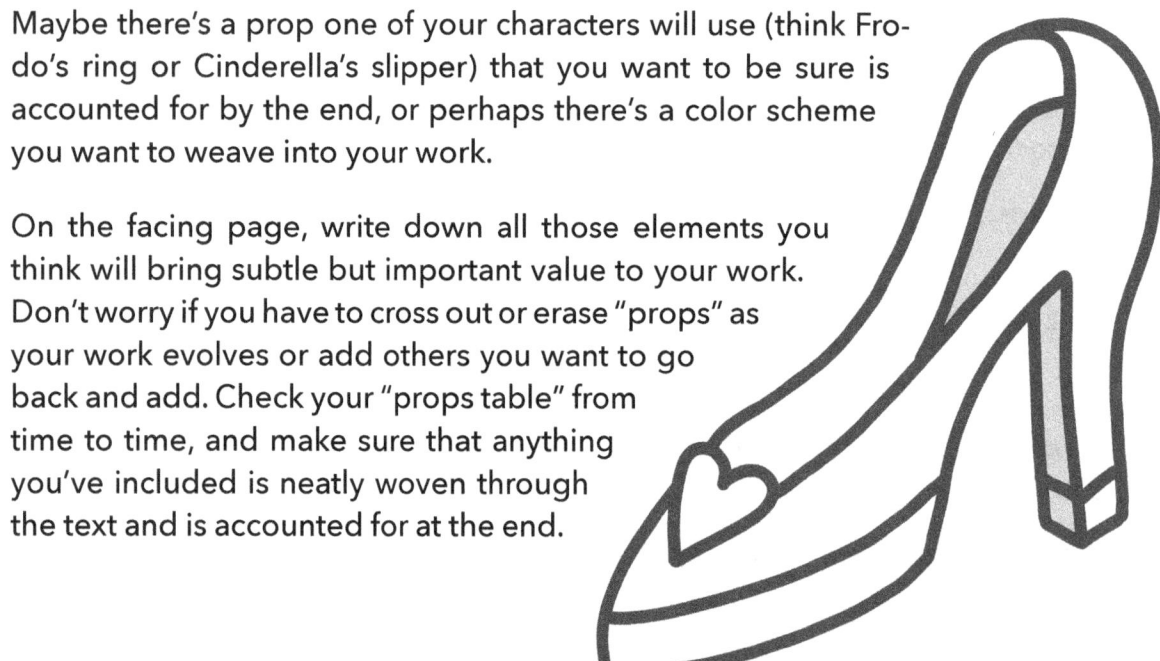

Embrace the Sloth

Sloths are cute, aren't they? You know why they move so slowly? Their metabolic rate is *extremely* slow. Compare that to hummingbirds, who have the quickest metabolism of all animals. We humans are somewhere in the middle, but that doesn't mean there won't be days when our fingers blur across the keyboard like a hummingbird's wings, while other days, simply stringing two words together feels like An. Enormous. Effort.

On those days, give yourself permission to embrace your inner sloth and conserve your energy. If you force the writing when you really don't want to be doing it, it can take the creativity out of it. So just do what you can. Even if it's just doodling.

This spread is for those sloth days. Just doodle! Embrace your inner sloth by doodling very slowly.

Envision This

A vision board is a visual representation of your dreams and goals. The idea is that looking at it daily will reaffirm your intention to manifest what you desire and spark the motivation you need to take action. It's also a message to the universe that this is what you want.

While vision boards are sometimes created for acquiring material things, like a new car or house or yacht, or for reaching goals, like climbing the ladder of success or running a marathon, or creating an ideal future, you can create a vision board to represent your writer's life—the way you *want* it to be.

To do this activity, you'll need a pile of old magazines and catalogs and/or electronic images and quotes you can print out, a piece of poster board, and a glue stick. (Go ahead and use a corkboard and pins if you don't like gluing.) Set aside a few hours for this activity so that you have time to really immerse yourself in the creation process.

So, what does your ideal writer's life look like to you? Think outside the box. It doesn't have to be a photo of you typing. Whatever images and words you choose, give yourself a real explanation of why you want those things and how they will benefit you.

- Choose images of your ideal writing space—an office overlooking a brilliant view from a big picture window? A cozy spot at the local coffee shop? A room set aside in your home with a big comfy couch, oak desk, and ergonomic office chair, etc.?

- Choose images the feeling of writing in the zone elicits—a majestic mountain, a babbling brook, a zen garden, etc.

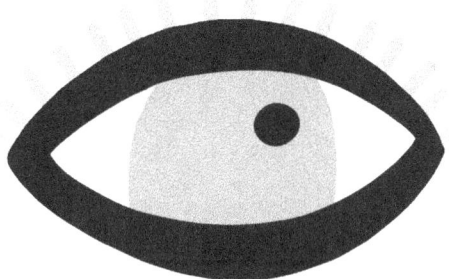

- Choose images of your ideal readers, reading books.
- Want to be a bestseller? Use a graphic of a bestseller award.
- Choose images in your usual genre. For example: Romance? Find an image of lovers embracing. Horror? Think zombies, skeletons, and spooky houses.
- Find photos of bookstores where you want your book to be on sale or images of the magazines or journals you want your article to appear in.
- Choose photos of people you can relate to who seem to be enjoying the success you want for yourself.
- Find positive quotes that inspire you to write. Maybe you'll come across some in this book. It's OK. You can cut them out. This is your book. Or just copy them down if cutting up a perfectly fine book isn't your thing.

Display your vision board somewhere you can look at it daily. Whenever it catches your eye, take a moment or two to study it and bring your intention to the forefront of your mind. The more you focus on your intention, the stronger your commitment to seeing it through will become.

Reset the Mood

Maybe you're feeling blocked because next up on your agenda is a cheerful scene or a positive topic and the weather has been particularly dreary. Or maybe you had an argument with a coworker and now that party scene or cheerful advice about getting along with others just annoys the heck out of you instead. Or perhaps you need to write a moving death scene for a beloved character, but you're just so darn happy you can't access those heart-wrenching feelings you want to impart to your readers.

A vision board is for inspiration and motivation, while a mood board is for . . . well, establishing a mood and theme.

Consider creating a mood board for each of the common feelings we humans experience—happiness, sadness, anger, romance, terror, serenity, and so on. Include images and words that evoke those feelings in you. For example, a "Happy" board might be full of yellows and oranges, pictures of flowers or animals that make you smile, etc., while a "Sad" board might be shades of gray with images of wilted flowers and storm clouds.

Then, when what you want to write just isn't matching your mood, pull out your mood board for that feeling. You can get really elaborate with this as a creative but brain-soothing exercise, or you can simply scroll through images from an internet search to access the feelings you need to write about.

▶ **TIP:** Appropriate music can set the mood, too!

The Writing Spider

The yellow garden spider, *Argiope aurantia,* is sometimes called the writing spider. Assuming you don't have arachnophobia, finding one of these spiders in your backyard can be a good omen. Heck, turning to this page in the book can also be a good omen of words to come!

In Native American lore, Spider wove the first alphabet in her web, and Spider represents infinite creativity. As you color the spider on the right, set an intention to channel Spider energy.

Good Reads

List three of your favorite books, and name three qualities you love about each one—like "witty dialogue" or "in-depth research" or "life-changing message."

1. _____ by _____

What I love about it: _____, _____, _____

2. _____ by _____

What I love about it: _____, _____, _____

3. _____ by _____

What I love about it: _____, _____, _____

Are these qualities you want to incorporate into your own writing? Are these old conventions of your genre that you'd like to flip on their heads? Are any of them already in your writing, but you've never realized it until now? Are any of them "guilty pleasure" elements you want to avoid? Spend a few minutes considering how each of these relates to your own work.

★ **Bonus:** Reread a favorite book! You'd be surprised what reading someone else's good writing can do for your writing mojo.

"The secret of getting ahead is getting started. The secret of getting started is breaking your complex overwhelming tasks into small manageable tasks, and then starting on the first one." ~Mark Twain*

*Whoa! Although this quote is often attributed to Mark Twain, arguably one of the greatest American writers of all time, there's no proof it's correctly attributed. There's a good lesson here: *Always check your sources.* But whatever the case may be, this is great advice.

Your Writing To-Do List

Maybe you want to write a 1,500-word article, a 3,000-word essay, a 65,000-word self-help book, a 100,000-word novel, or some other fantastic piece of writing. That's the *goal*—not the first item on your to-do list.

Break up the writing process into chunks: Need to gather research? Put that at the top of your list. Have a deadline? Put "set up a schedule to produce X number of words by X date" on your list. Work best with an outline? Add that to your list as well. Need to create a first draft of your introduction or chapter 1? You get the idea. Break the goal into smaller action steps you can do one at a time.

Start brainstorming your to-do list here and then copy it over to a word-processing document, print it out, and check off the items as you go. Be sure to set a realistic timeframe to accomplish each subgoal.

1. _____

2. _____

3. _____

4. _____

5. _____

In Search of Words

Searching for the perfect words, but nothing's coming to you right now? Give your creative mind a break by searching for these writerly words in this word search puzzle. After you do this puzzle, get back to your real-life word search. As you do, imagine that as you scan your brain for the hidden words, they just start popping up.

AUTHORSHIP	EDIT	OUTLINE
BOOK	FINALIZE	PARAPHRASE
COMMUNICATION	GRAMMAR	PUBLISH
COMPOSE	ILLUSTRATE	READ
COMPOSITION	KNOWLEDGE	READERS
CONTEXTUALIZE	LANGUAGE	REWRITE
DRAFT	MANUSCRIPT	STORYTELLING
EBOOK	MEDIA	VOCABULARY

(The solution's on page 296.)

```
H N S O J M Y D E C R I B E X A F L M F L C G S E Z H V Q A
M X I X P D V Y L K E Z D W O I T F R M D D A K M H P Y L P
H Z N O I V S A C U J X K Z P S V R O L U U O C M O R F O W
N K L X M O N T A R Q R T V J E G D E L W O N K E D I T A F
O K A G U G F I W E H F D X U F H S T V Y P A B Q S F P R J
S X B P U R S L C I Z H L X C X W O X B I D B I C I Z P O K
Q O V A M U G D U E W A E K E S S R H S I B M C D W G E P A
X K G V M H D E C A A P P W C N C B S G P L R T W E O O L Q
M E S F H T O X V M O H B O O O C C I X J C K G Q J M J E S
E I H S I L B U P H Z Z M Z K O O B G B N L N R L W N D H U
Q Z P T J D L F M E I P C X Z S Y W I J S W Z S E K K W E D
H I I Q T H P U M C O X E G T Y T Q N G J A V G Y W Y B J B
T T Y L T G O P L S Z B G O S P E T O C H E Y Z F K R J A D
X U J I A H Q D I C V Y R J I O G J I J R L X R M X E I A C
H K X K P N A T I K W Y C R E Y I C T V Z W W R Y D S E T V
D I A N D E I P A Z T G C O S Z R O A M C A I V C S R E E E
P Y S D C O N F V E W S S V A Y Z N C K A Y I N Y A E E Q R
J B U C N B O I L J U H J M R P X T I F T K A T G U Y X G H
M M V R O N K L L N B I N V H N X E N P U P M U O I P D C Q
E S L T C M I T A T Q L T V P O C X U V R A M M A R G X F R
T Z V C L N P M O Y U J F O A F R T M U A J T D M Y O X K S
A F T Y G W N O A E H O A C R C S U M R N J D M Q X X O Y H
R V G K O M D R S G Z F R A A W P A O S Y R W F Q E Y X D B
T N B F G C X U M E C T D B P B P L C W K L Z Z J N K J Z R
S I R P E F W M P F H G A U F B V I S O L C W D K N B H E R
U G K B Q T Y D R W O I E L B T J Z P U E K T S R E D A E R
L T A N A P M U D J H I B A Z U S E O T H Z S Y G Z G A E M
L M S V T S X Y W H O R O R K M G Y O Z U P M I L P G U P B
I Q P I H S R O H T U A O Y X E Z H A B M T J T A U W I Q Z
G F R E Z Z Q U L K D K K K T B M V K D W L H L M P W O F C
```

Set a Target

To give your mind some direction, have a general idea of your total target word count (it helps to know the average word range in your genre), and set a realistic date in the future when you want or need to complete the first draft—perhaps six months or a year from now. Divide your target word count by the time between now and that future date (e.g., to write a 60,000-word manuscript in 12 months, you'll need to produce 5,000 words per month).

With that number in mind, set a target word count for your writing sessions. Using the above target example, if you write five days a week for two hours per day, you would target about at least 250 words per session (in this case, an average double-spaced page). You may, of course, write more than that (fingers crossed). It's just your minimum target. Here's the calculation:

Target word count: _____ divided by _____ weeks to complete = _____ words to produce each week divided by ____ days of the week = _____ daily target word count

Here's an example:

>24,000 words / 6 weeks = 4,000 / 5 days = 800 words daily target word count

Now, you may be thinking, *But when I'm in the zone, I can write 2,500 words a day.* Fantastic—you'll be ahead of schedule and have plenty of time for revisions! You'll also have a little downtime when you need it.

Here it is again:

Target word count: _____ divided by _____ weeks to complete = _____ words to produce each week divided by ____ days of the week = _____ daily target word count

You'll probably want to pull out your calculator for this. But if you're old school, here's some graph paper:

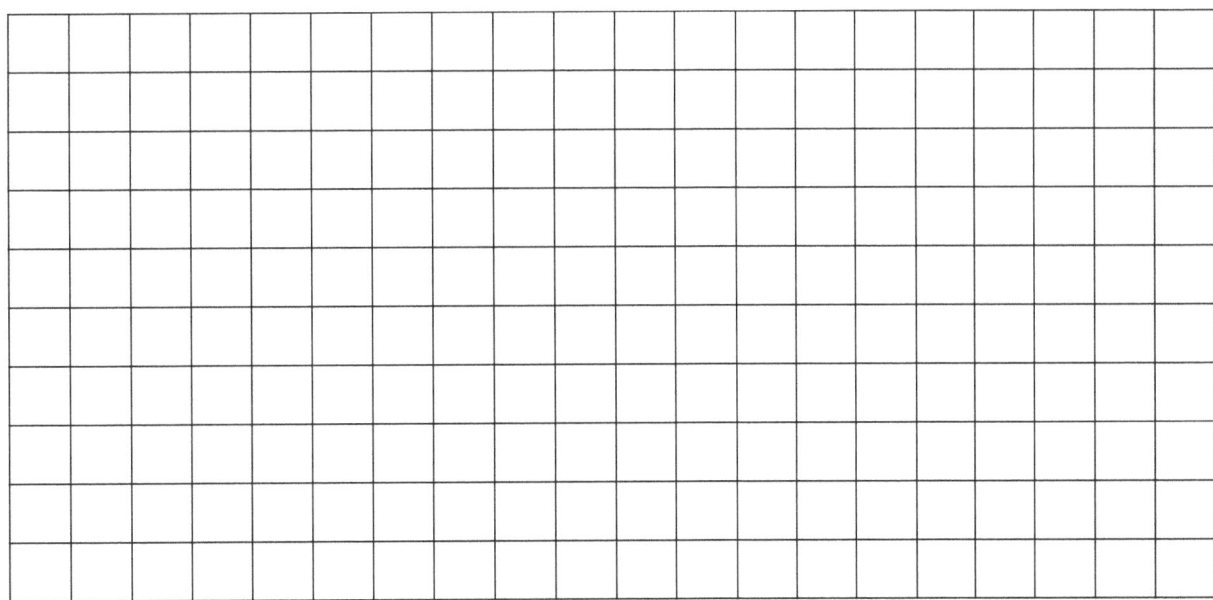

"When it is obvious that the goals cannot be reached, don't adjust the goals, adjust the action steps."
~Confucius

Move the Target

Do you have a target word count you just can't seem to reach every day? Do you see other writers progressing at a pace you only wish you could match? Sometimes the writing process just seems to drag, and it's harder to feel like writing when everyone else seems more motivated than you are.

Despite what a fortune cookie might advise you, if you can't hit your target word count, move the target closer. Maybe you can't do 800 words a day, but if you consistently hit around 600, make 500 your target word count. That will put less pressure on you, and every writing day will feel like a good one!

Remember to adjust the finish line, too. You can always reset it if your words flow more quickly.

My new target daily word count is: _____.

Make a Pledge

Writing something other people want to read isn't for those who lack determination. It's hard work that requires consistent and persistent effort. Yes, it can also be fun and rewarding, but it doesn't come without some struggles, challenges, and lots of compromise.

If you haven't done so already, it's time to commit yourself to putting in the time it takes to produce a good piece of writing. In the space below, make a pledge to yourself that you will see this process through, whatever it takes.

I pledge to: _____

_____

_____

_____

_____

_____

_____

_____

_____

_____

Read a Book

Some writers won't read works that are similar to what they're currently working on because they don't want to be influenced, consciously or subconsciously, by what they read. When you're in the thick of things (like making *real* progress), that makes sense.

But that's probably not the case right now. Hopefully, you've already spent many hours reading books or articles you think would resonate with your "ideal readers." This type of research gives you a good idea of what your readers expect—even if you decide to throw all that out in your own work.

If you haven't done your "reading research," now's the time to create a reading list of at least four titles and choose a title among them to read now. Poke around and look for noteworthy titles in your genre, and then record those titles here:

1. _____
2. _____
3. _____
4. _____

On the other hand, if you've read all you can to prepare for your own work, read outside your genre. Want to catch two butterflies with one net? Read a book on creativity.

> "Read a thousand books, and your words will flow like a river." ~Lisa See

What Can You See?

Pareidolia is an imagined perception of a meaningful image or pattern in an ambiguous shape, like looking at the clouds and seeing a dragon blowing smoke or a pod of whales swimming through the sky. While the well-known Rorschach test might be used to psychoanalyze someone, looking for and identifying "hidden" images and meanings in things like inkblots, clouds, and coffee spilled across your desk doesn't mean you're crazy; it means you're creative. (In the case of the coffee, maybe a little messy, too.)

> *Take a deep breath, set a timer for 5 minutes, and simply look at the inkblot. See into it. Find the meaning that emerges in your mind through the splatter. Write about it if you feel inspired to, or just take note of what comes into your mind.*

_____

_____

_____

_____

_____

Next time you're outside (or go outside now), spend some time looking up at the clouds. Let the images and the stories surrounding them appear to you. You don't have to do anything with what comes up. This is a simple creativity exercise to get your mind used to the idea of creating something from "nothing."

Take an Elephant Break

Have you ever been up close and personal with an elephant? If so, you have an idea of their powerful presence. What if you could harness that power to crush your Writer's Block?

Imagine that your Writer's Block is in the path of a charging elephant. And *BAM!*—that obstacle is suddenly trampled into a thousand useless pieces. (Be sure to get out of the way!)

Now, bring the elephant on the facing page to life by coloring it in. As you do, think about what you want to write about when you next put your pen to paper or your fingers to keyboard.

"The greater the obstacle, the more glory in overcoming it."
~Molière

Alphabet Ransom

The 26 letters of the alphabet are scattered across these pages in no particular order or pattern. Write a word or phrase that begins with each letter as you encounter it on the page. If you can't think of something that starts with that letter, skip it and circle back. This simple exercise gives your creative mind an easy workout. (You can bench-press heavier weights later.)

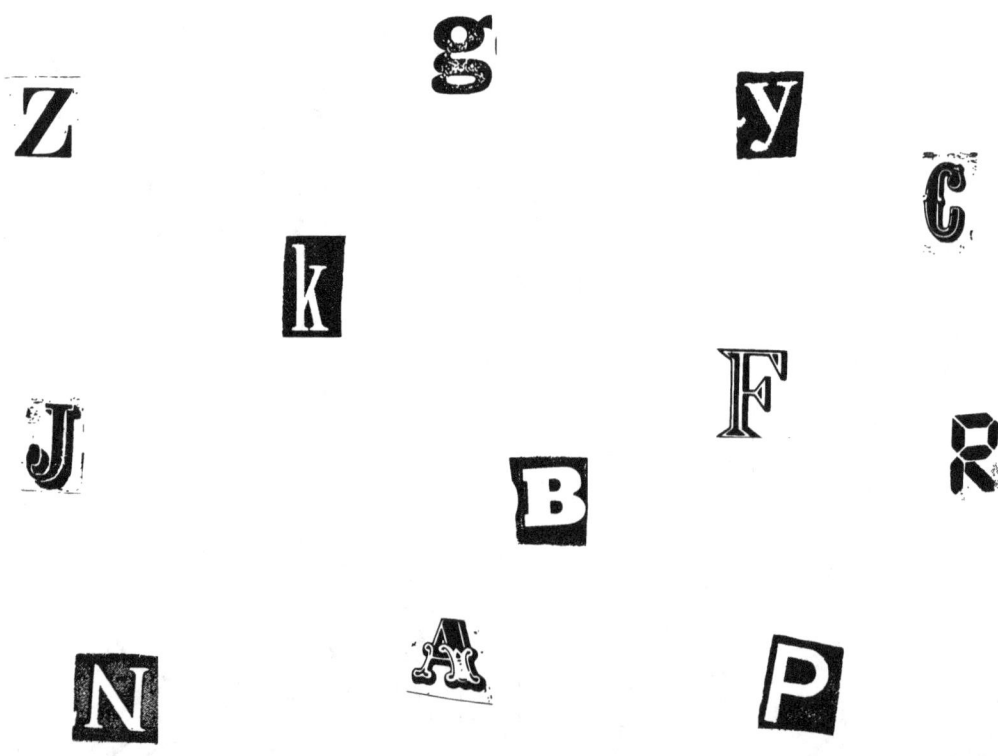

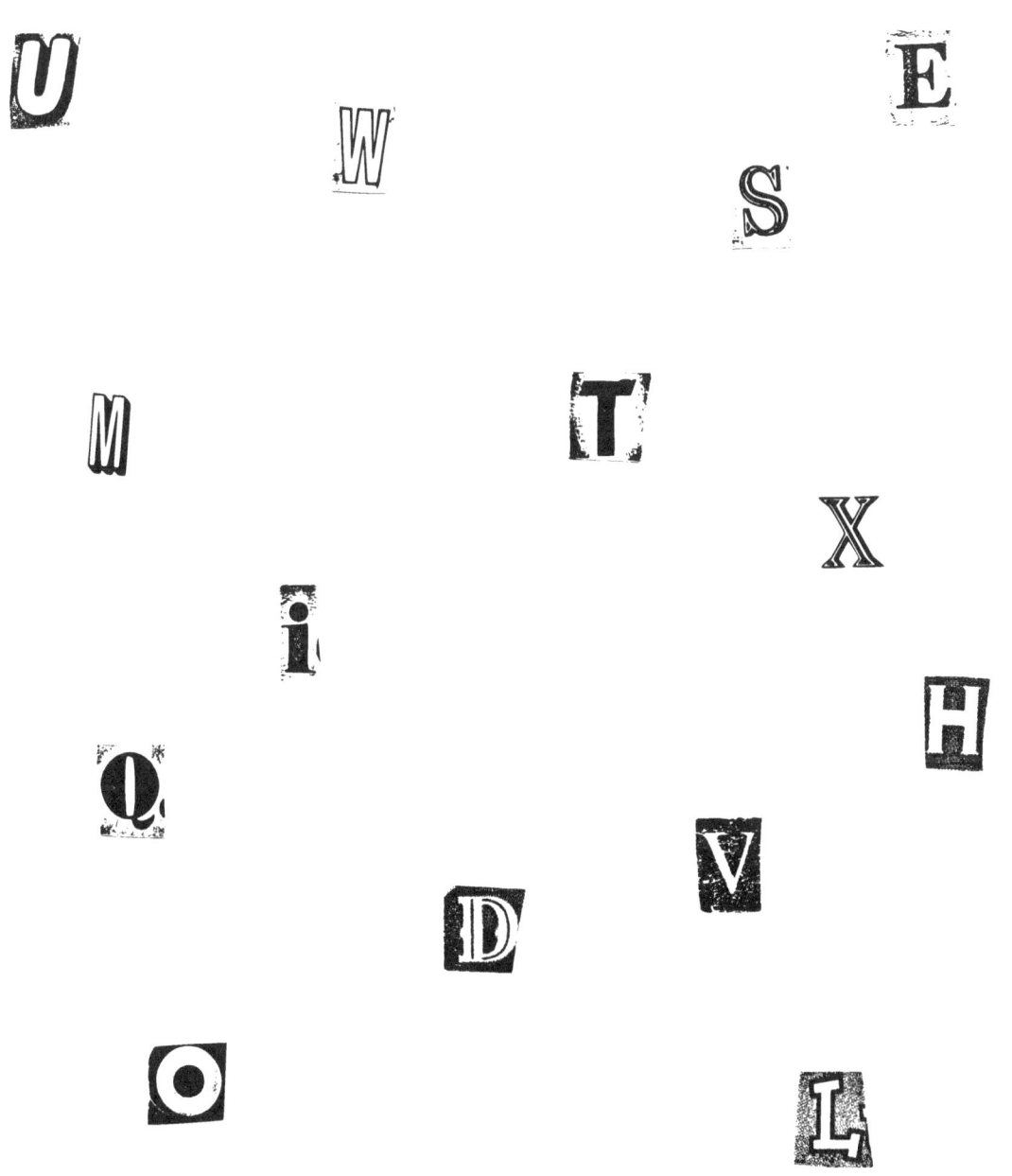

Brain Freeze

Are you feeling frazzled because you've been overworking yourself? Maybe your brain is on the fritz and you just need to reboot it like you would your smartphone when an app freezes. How? Turn it "off" by giving it a break from producing words—or at least trying to.

Here are some ways to "reboot" your brain (no creativity required; in fact, avoid it).

- Take a 20-minute power nap.
- Go for a bike ride around the neighborhood.
- Relax in a bathtub or take an invigorating shower.
- Drink a cup of tea without doing anything else.
- Listen to a guided meditation or hypnosis.
- Take your dog to the park. (No dog? Take yourself there.)
- Hit the local gym.
- Color the image on the facing page using different shades of blue.
- Get a good night's sleep.

Revisit the Past

Think of one life-changing event from your past. Set your timer for 15 minutes and describe the event on the facing page.

Now skip to one of the blanks in the back of this book and, in those same 15 minutes, describe the same event a second time without trying to repeat what you wrote the first time. Just start again.

When you're done, compare the two. You probably already did, but if you didn't, don't peek at the upside-down text below until you've completed both paragraphs.

> "You don't start out writing good stuff. You start out writing crap and thinking it's good stuff, and then gradually you get better at it. That's why I say one of the most valuable traits is persistence." ~Octavia E. Butler

*Bet you noticed that your writing evolved from one version to the next. That's because the first time around was practice.

Stephy's Dilemma

This easy-level logic problem offers your creative mind a little respite while still giving your brain a good workout. By the way, if you can solve logic problems like this one, you can certainly solve your Writer's Block.

Stephy is the new editorial director at a publishing house, and she has four books to assign to the four editors on her staff, each of whom has a specialty. The deadlines for the projects range from 1 to 4 months. She took notes during a staff meeting, but now looking at her notes, she's not sure who should get which project or what the timeline is for each manuscript. Can you help here? Here are her notes:

- This will not be Sarah's first project with a deadline that's longer than 10 weeks.
- Fantasy never takes fewer than 10 weeks, and self-motivation never needs more than 5 weeks.
- The person who works on business manuscripts needs the most time.
- Carol can't sustain her attention on a project for more than four weeks.
- The fantasy editor will complain that they didn't get as much time as at least one of the other editors.
- Michael and the fantasy editor sometimes collaborate.
- Gary reads espionage for pleasure, which is why he doesn't edit that genre.
- Sarah is not interested in working on business books.

	Self-motivation	Espionage	Fantasy	Business	1	2	3	4
Carol								
Gary								
Sarah								
Michael								
1								
2								
3								
4								

INSTRUCTIONS: The list of clues (Stephy's notes) correspond to the four categories (the genres) and the two items that fall into each category (the editor and timelines). Each item can be matched to only one category. Your job is to deduce from the clues which items match which category to help Stephy out. Use Xs to block out the boxes in the grid for items that don't match the category based on the clues. Block out the boxes in the grid for items that don't pair up, too. When all the items but one in a grid is crossed out, that box aligns with the category or item. Still have no idea how to approach this? Do an internet search for "how to solve a logic problem." ☺

"In descriptions of Nature one must seize on small details, grouping them so that when the reader closes his eyes he gets a picture. For instance, you'll have a moonlit night if you write that on the mill dam a piece of glass from a broken bottle glittered like a bright little star." ~Anton Chekhov

Show Me

Here's a good brain workout: Look up from this book and notice the first thing you see. Choose a few words to describe the object and its location. For the next 5 minutes, brainstorm other ways to impart to the reader the position and qualities of the object without using your original descriptors or naming the item and setting directly.

Hate to ♥ It?

Many artists have a love-hate relationship with their craft, writers included. In fact, several famous writers have likened the writing process to sweating blood or opening a vein. Wow. They must've *really* loved it. What's your relationship with writing? Think about it for a moment and then "bleed" into the space provided:

What do you love most about writing?

_____

_____

What do you hate most about writing?

Writer's Block. (There, I wrote it for you. Think of something else.)

_____

_____

> "Writing is not necessarily something to be ashamed of, but do it in private and wash your hands afterwards." ~Robert A. Heinlein

In the Write Mind

Have you prepared your mind for your writing session, or did you just flop down in front of the computer hoping the words would come? Preparation, they say, is everything, so if you haven't prepared your mind for the task at hand, set a timer for 5 minutes and do the following:

1. Sit comfortably in your chair with your feet on the floor and hands in your lap or on your armrests. Close your eyes or gaze softly ahead of you at a point on the wall.

2. Take a deep breath in through your nose and let it out through your mouth, three times. Then breathe as you naturally would. Say to your mind, "Mind, it's time for us to write. But first, let's get clear."

3. Let your mind wander as it will, but don't pay any attention to it. Don't try to hold on to or respond to a thought. See each thought scroll away as if you are mentally swiping down on a social-media newsfeed without stopping to comment or tap "like, love, care, haha, wow, sad, or angry." Just keep scrolling until the timer chimes.

4. Now, take three more breaths, and remind your mind once more that it's time to write.

If this meditation works for you, do it before each writing session. If it didn't, give it a few tries before you abandon it. Scrolling through your mind feed without commenting or reacting to the thoughts you'll find there takes practice.

After the Introductions . . .

Your small boat capsizes, and you find yourself stranded on a sunny tropical island with only the drenched clothes on your back and one sneaker on your foot. A man with a long beard wearing a green cape, a woman with a piña colada and an umbrella, and a small child holding a white-faced capuchin by its tiny hand greet you at the shore. Once the usual pleasantries are past, what does each character warn you about the island? (Yes, the monkey can speak.)

It was the best of words.
It was the worst of words.

What is your favorite word? _____

What is your least favorite word? _____

    If those words were characters in a story, what would they talk about?

_____
_____
_____
_____
_____
_____
_____
_____
_____

Ho Hum

Lacking interest in what you're writing? Maybe it's something you *must* get done, like a paper for school or something work-related. If it's a creative piece that you have no interest in right now, maybe you've been working on it "too long" without a break or maybe it's time to file it away and write something else.

Figuring out *why* you're bored is just one piece of the puzzle. If you simply need to get something done, your best bet is to push through it and get your first draft on paper. Maybe you'll find the editing process more engaging.

If you simply must write something that you have little interest in, keep your eye on the prize that comes with the finished piece, and give yourself little rewards along the way at set intervals. For example, write for 30 minutes or produce 250 words, give yourself a reward such as:

- ★ A piece of that candy bar you stashed in your desk drawer.
- ★ A quick scroll through social media.
- ★ A fresh cup of coffee.
- ★ A brief chat with a friend.
- ★ A 5-minute power nap.

Avoid getting so caught up in your reward that you abandon your project for greener pastures. These are little rewards, and they're meant to keep you going, not derail you.

"If I waited for perfection,
I would never write a word."
~Margaret Atwood

Perfect the Art of Imperfection

Perfection—complete freedom from fault or defect—simply isn't attainable in this earthly realm. Why? Because perfection is subjective, so one person's concept of "perfect" can be entirely different from someone else's. This rule applies to art, literature included.

If you struggle with perfection, there's a good chance you're still on your first draft, maybe even your first paragraph. Let's face it, the first draft is the hardest precisely because it is so, well, imperfect. But you can't make something better if there's *nothing* to make better.

Struggling to create a polished piece of writing the first time around is like expecting to play violin in the New York Philharmonic after just a couple lessons. So, make an agreement with yourself to be perfectly imperfect as you write here:

I agree to: _____

_____

_____

Tell yourself right now that your writing doesn't have to be perfect, and you don't have to be perfect. Have you done that? Yes? Perfect.

You are enough.

Not Feeling "Good Enough"?

Virtually all writers struggle with not feeling good enough from time to time. It's human nature to sometimes question our abilities. But what if you really don't feel like a good writer, but you desperately want to write? What if this feeling is keeping you from putting fingers to keyboard or completing the great idea you started?

Take a writing course. Google "writing courses," and you'll find at least 1.7 billion options to choose from. Of course, you'll need to separate the wheat from the chaff to find the best fit for you, but do it. If you truly want to write, develop the skills you need to make it happen. Your confidence will grow, and so will your word count.

With that said, do be sure you're not being too hard on yourself. Remember, lots of people struggle with feelings of inadequacy on occasion. The best course of action is to keep "practicing" (that is, writing). With practice comes improvement. In the end, that nagging feeling that you can do better might be just what you need to keep honing your craft.

Inside-Out Perspective

When you're used to looking at the world as one way or another—as in bad or good, up or down, beautiful or ugly, this or that, positive or negative, probable or improbable—you cannot access the many other possibilities that exist outside a black-or-white perspective. A limited view can create obstacles to finding a sense of freshness in your writing.

You can start opening your mind by first turning everything inside out and seeing it for its opposite. Here's a little practice prompt:

> *Name something (object, place, person, or concept) you normally consider ugly, like **really** ugly. Your job now is to describe its unparalleled beauty with conviction:*

Classical Boost

Classical music is full of energy and emotion, and it's known for boosting brainpower and creativity. So, get comfortable, put your earbuds in, and choose one of the handpicked pieces on the facing page. Plug it into your music app or on YouTube.

1. Close your eyes, and as you listen, allow the music to tell you a story through your emotions and imagination, without forcing anything.

2. Let the thoughts and feelings simply wash over you.

3. After you've listened to the whole piece, play it again, but this time with your fingers on the keyboard and your cursor flashing.

4. Write to the tempo of the music ANYTHING you are moved to write.

5. Don't worry about punctuation, grammar, or misspellings—just keep going until the composition ends.

The *Brandenburg Concertos* (Bach)

Piano Concerto No. 5 in D, K. 175 (Mozart)

Prelude to the Afternoon of a Faun (Debussy)

"Overture" from *The Flying Dutchman* (Wagner)

Symphony No. 9 in D Minor, Op. 125 (Beethoven)

"The Garland Waltz" from *The Sleeping Beauty* (Tchaikovsky)

Rhapsody on a Theme of Paganini, Op. 43 (Rachmaninoff)

Symphony No. 3 in F major, Op. 90 (Brahms)

Polonaise in A-flat major, Op. 53 (Chopin)

Cello Concerto No 2 in D major (Haydn)

The Four Seasons (Vivaldi)

"I would rather write 10,000 notes than a single letter of the alphabet."
~Ludwig van Beethoven

20 Get-Writing Prompts

Sometimes responding to a writing prompt, even if it has nothing to do with what you *want* to write, can help get your creative juices flowing hard and fast enough to wash away your Writer's Block. Take a stab at one of these 20 writing prompts. Set a time limit (a half hour, maybe) and a word limit (150, 300, or 500 words) and explore the images, scenarios, settings, and feelings that the prompt elicits.

1. The tabby and the gecko in the kitchen
2. Your extraterrestrial classmate or coworker
3. The blue sock with a hole in the sole
4. An abandoned bicycle on the side of the road
5. The night the lights went out in the superstore
6. Training two hyper puppies at once
7. Assembling a swing set without instructions
8. Exploring a deep, dark cave
9. What dinosaur skeletons do when the museum is closed
10. What the yarn said to the knitting needles
11. A classic book meets a newly published one in the bookstore
12. Adventures of a lost marble
13. Condiment conference in the back of the fridge
14. The perfect day
15. What the people in a painting are thinking
16. A tightrope walker's first preperformance jitters
17. What a car thinks when it goes through the car wash
18. How a guitar feels when it's being restrung
19. Looking for a lost set of keys
20. Getting lost in the woods

Your Weekly Planner

Do you wait for the desire and drive to write to overtake you? That's how some writers write their best work. They write when they feel called to—even if it's 2 a.m. They are not the ones with the Writer's Block. At least not at the moment. For others, having a writing schedule can make all the difference between producing nothing and getting thoughts on paper.

The obstacle you're facing now might not be a lack of ideas but rather unstructured writing habits. Your brain may have no idea it's time to produce words if it doesn't know *when* it's supposed to do that.

Look at your typical week. Which days and what blocks of time will you set aside for working on your manuscript? If you have a day job, this might mean some earlier mornings or later nights or lunchbreaks with your laptop. Maybe you can work for longer stretches on your days off. Maybe you have a lot of flexibility and can write whenever you want. (Even if that's the case, block off specific days and times to keep you and your brain on the same page.)

Setting aside time and actually scheduling it into your calendar reaffirms your commitment to write. It means forgoing other plans during the times you have set aside to write.

Be realistic when it comes to creating your writing schedule. Telling yourself you'll write for five hours a day seven days a week when you really only have two hours to yourself sets you up for failure. But do schedule writing sessions as frequently as you reasonably can because the forward momentum will keep you motivated and focused.

Week of: _____

Writing Goals for the Week: _____
_____
_____

MONDAY
☐ DAY OFF ☐ WRITING DAY

Session 1: _____ to _____

Additional sessions:

_____ to _____

_____ to _____

TUESDAY
☐ DAY OFF ☐ WRITING DAY

Session 1: _____ to _____

Additional sessions:

_____ to _____

_____ to _____

WEDNESDAY
☐ DAY OFF ☐ WRITING DAY

Session 1: _____ to _____

Additional sessions:

_____ to _____

_____ to _____

THURSDAY
☐ DAY OFF ☐ WRITING DAY

Session 1: _____ to _____

Additional sessions:

_____ to _____

_____ to _____

FRIDAY
☐ DAY OFF ☐ WRITING DAY

Session 1: _____ to _____

Additional sessions:

_____ to _____

_____ to _____

SATURDAY
☐ DAY OFF ☐ WRITING DAY

Session 1: _____ to _____

Additional sessions:

_____ to _____

_____ to _____

SUNDAY
☐ DAY OFF ☐ WRITING DAY

Session 1: _____ to _____

Additional sessions:

_____ to _____

_____ to _____

Notes: _____
_____
_____
_____
_____
_____

Power-Up Phrase

Traditionally, a mantra is repeated to aid a meditator's concentration. In some circles, *mantra* has become synonymous with *affirmation* (think: *I can accomplish anything I set my mind to*). What's common among both is that they give your mind something to focus on instead of all those potentially creativity-blocking voices in your head. They essentially "reset" your mind, giving you back your brainpower. When your mind is back in your control, you can guide it toward what you want (that is, to write) instead of what you don't want (Writer's Block).

Come up with a phrase that has meaning to you that you can repeat to yourself at least five times. When your mind starts wandering away from the page and toward your insecurities or to-do list, take back your power by reminding your mind to behave with this simple phrase. Here are a couple ideas:

- *My mind works for me, and right now, we are writing.*
- *Good prose flows effortlessly from my fingertips.*
- *I am writing, and my mind is full of engaging ideas.*

This phrase can be anything that works for you. If it powers you up to get you back writing and puts you in the mood to write, then it's a good phrase.

Write your power-up phrase here: _____

_____

_____

As you color in the peacock, repeat your phrase to yourself. Mythologically speaking, Peacocks symbolize power.

Chase Those Cares Away

Some poets produce their best work when they're sad. That's sort of sad in itself. But it's true: Grief, isolation, disappointment, hurt, melancholy, and a host of other "unhappy" emotions are often the subject of deeply meaningful writing. These are feelings we can all relate to at one time or another, and perhaps we seek solace in others' similar experiences.

However, a general feeling of unhappiness may actually be what's keeping you from writing in the first place. If you are so unhappy that you simply cannot get what's in your head out on paper or come up with new ideas, maybe it's time to speak to someone about what's causing your unhappiness. A good friend or a therapist may be your best next stop.

With that said, if you're simply feeling blue and want a quick pick-me-up so you can get back to writing your masterpiece, here are some good ideas:

- Watch a comedy you've never seen before—the dumber the better.
- Watch funny animal videos—but don't fall down the rabbit hole; set a time limit.
- Do something silly, like wearing socks on your hands, as you go about your morning routine.
- Play your favorite song, stand in front of the mirror, and "practice" dancing.
- Go see a comedian or watch one on video.
- Read comic strips. (*Calvin and Hobbes* is my all-time favorite).

A Momentary Reset

Let's say you're sitting down to write. Your fingers touch the keyboard and your mind goes blank. Suddenly you're in a panic. Now's a good time to bring yourself back to the present with a body awareness exercise that involves all five of your senses, plus one.

Take a deep breath and then answer each of the following questions in order in your mind, taking enough time to really experience each sensation:

1. What do you hear? For example, the wind shaking the windowpanes or the hum of your computer.

2. What do you see? For example, a flashing cursor, your laptop, or a bottle of water.

3. What are you touching? For example, the keyboard or the arms of your chair.

4. What are you tasting? For example, you last sip of coffee or the onions you had with lunch.

5. What are you smelling? For example, the candle you were burning to set the mood or the shampoo you used this morning.

6. What are you sensing? In other words, what thoughts or feelings have come to the surface? Acknowledge whatever it is, thank them for making their presence known, and tell them you are ready to write and ask them to please not distract you for the time being.

7. Take another breath. Hopefully, you've been breathing the whole time, but now make it an intentional cleansing breath and get back to writing.

Tapping into your senses is a great way to cut out the noise of everyday life, reset your mind, and hit the page writing!

Professional Feedback

Some people are in the business of improving a writer's material, whether through critical feedback or directly modifying the material. They're called editors (which sounds scarier than it is). As a writer, you should have at least one trusted professional editor you can turn to.

If you're having trouble moving forward with something you've written, maybe you just need a fresh pair of professional eyes to look it over and offer you some insight. Perhaps your editor can pinpoint your blind spots so that you can move forward with renewed vision and know-how.

Look for an editor with traditional publishing experience. A good editor can help you identify what's working and what's not. They can also help you tailor your work to your target audience so that it can be more competitive in a saturated market.

"You write to communicate to the hearts and minds of others what's burning inside you, and we edit to let the fire show through the smoke." ~Arthur Plotnik

Filling in the Gaps

Good chance you're familiar with this childhood word-swap activity, which is always fun to do no matter how old you are. On this page, you'll write a word in the prompts without looking ahead, and on the next page, you'll fill them in the lines where prompted. Why? Because it's fun, and a little fun every now and again can give your brain a much-needed break.

Adjective _____

A topic _____

Past-tense verb _____

Adjective _____

A feeling _____

A number _____

Ordinal number _____

Adjective _____

Adverb _____

Color _____

Adjective _____

A feeling _____

Past-tense verb _____

Interjection _____

Adjective ending in "er" _____

Number _____

Professional title _____

Interjection _____

Plural noun _____

Name of a newspaper
    or magazine _____

A feeling _____

83

Directions: Using the words you entered on the previous page, fill in the blanks.

Best-Selling Hit

I decided to write a/an _____ book about _____. So I
                                ADJECTIVE   A TOPIC

_____ on my _____ computer and got down to work.
PAST-TENSE VERB   ADJECTIVE

I felt _____, but I knew I could do it.
        A FEELING

_____ days later, I finished my _____ draft. My _____ editor
NUMBER   ORDINAL NUMBER   ADJECTIVE

marked it up _____ with a _____ pen. The _____
              ADVERB   COLOR   ADJECTIVE

edits made me feel _____. I _____ through my revisions,
                    A FEELING   PAST-TENSE VERB

and _____, it was even _____ than when I'd started.
     INTERJECTION   ADJECTIVE ENDING IN "ER"

_____ months later, it got published by a _____. _____
NUMBER   PROFESSIONAL TITLE   INTERJECTION

for me! It was worth all the _____ I put in. My book made it to the
                              PLURAL NOUN

_____ bestseller list, and I felt _____!
NEWSPAPER OR MAGAZINE   A FEELING

10 Short Steps to Your Short Story

1. Pick a theme—for example, good versus evil, humanity versus nature, coming of age, corruption and power, grief and death, hero's journey (courage), individual versus society, love (friendship, romance, familial, etc.), poverty, prejudice, spirituality, rags to riches, survival, war . . .

2. Choose a familiar setting, both the starting point and any points along the way.

3. Identify and name your main character: person or animal, any age, any gender.

4. Create a problem or conflict your main character must solve by the end. Identify what brings this issue to the forefront in your character's mind.

5. Name the series of obstacles your character will face on the way to solve the problem, with the final obstacle the most difficult.

6. List the resources your character needs to solve the problem, and figure out how your character will gather those resources.

7. Name the side characters who will attempt to thwart your main character's efforts and why they want to stand in your character's way.

8. Name the side characters who will help your main character along and why they want to help.

9. Identify how the story will resolve.

10. Create a "story map" using all the information you've just gathered. Your story map should include a beginning, middle, and end. (You can have as many middles as you need to tell the complete story.)

Shades of Gray

Are you stuck in a black-or-white version of reality? It's time to don your "gray shades" and think outside the page. Expand your perspective by looking at your topic (or even the process of writing) from an opposite point of view.

1. Make a list of main points that support your perspective.

2. Now, take the opposite stance as if you were on both sides of a debate, and make a list of main points that support the flip side.

3. Now, this is key: Look at all the gray areas in between. Is there any overlap? Can a compromise be made to merge these different perspectives?

This exercise can add more depth to your writing because it allows you to see the other side of an argument and everything in between. For example, if you're trying to convince the reader that your character is making the right choice in a problematic scenario, flip the script to see how a reader might argue that same character is actually the villain in that same scenario.

If you can understand how a reader might interpret a scenario from a different angle, you can tweak your writing to strengthen your argument. Alternatively, if you'd like a character or plot point to land more in that gray area, seeing the two extremes can help you find the middle ground.

MAIN POINTS	SHADES OF GRAY	OPPOSITE VIEWS

"There are things known and there are things unknown, and in between are the doors of perception." ~Aldous Huxley

Debunk Your Inner Critic

Set a timer for 5 minutes. Freewrite the worst review you can about you as a writer—include all those negative beliefs you may have about yourself as a writer and your current work.

_____
_____
_____
_____
_____

After you've written the bad review, defend yourself and your work. For the next 5 minutes, come up with all the positive things you can say that debunk your critic's review.

_____
_____
_____
_____
_____

Debunk Your Inner Critic

Set a timer for 5 minutes. Freewrite the worst review you can about you as a writer—include all those negative beliefs you may have about yourself as a writer and your current work.

_____
_____
_____
_____
_____

After you've written the bad review, defend yourself and your work. For the next 5 minutes, come up with all the positive things you can say that debunk your critic's review.

_____
_____
_____
_____
_____

A Walk Around the Writer's Block

1. Give your Writer's Block a name.

2. Imagine he/she/it has short legs.

3. Get up and head to your front door, imagining that your Writer's Block is behind you, trying to keep up.

4. Be kind and hold the door open until your Writer's Block makes it outside.

5. Now, take a walk around the block.

6. Walk as quickly as you can, putting more and more distance between you and your Writer's Block.

7. By the time you make it back to your front door, your Writer's Block will be just halfway around the block. (Little legs, remember?)

8. Go inside, and lock the door. Start writing.

Then What Happened?

I went to the store, and I bought an alligator, baker's chocolate, candy corns, and ducklings. The ducklings ate all the candy corn, and then the alligator ripped through my shopping bag, scattering my purchases onto the sidewalk and into the street. The baker's chocolate melted on the hot pavement. The alligator lunged for one of the ducklings but slipped on the melted chocolate, and *that* duckling got away.

Silly? Yes. Does it conjure up images? Yes. That's the whole idea of this creativity exercise. If you can't think of the first line, use the "I went to the store" example starting with "E." Once you have your opening sentence, write a simple paragraph by asking yourself, "And then what happened?" after each sentence.

_____
_____
_____
_____
_____
_____
_____
_____

All Boxed In

Here's a cathartic exercise cleverly disguised as a craft project:

1. Head to the local craft store and pick up a paper box. You can also reuse an empty tissue box and remove any plastic film, or grab an old shoebox or other paperboard container.

2. Grab a sheet of paper (or two) and cut it into strips.

3. On each strip, write a perceived "obstacle" that stands between you and finishing your masterpiece.

4. One by one, read the strips and place them in the box.

5. When you're out of strips, take the box outside and stomp on it! Squash it, trample it—smash it with a hammer if you must! Then chuck it in the rubbish bin.

You'd be amazed how the symbolic destruction of those barriers can empower you to write again. Have fun stompin'!

Metaphorize It!

Simile compares attributes of two things, often using "like" or "as." Metaphor uses words in place of others to suggest similarity or to evoke a deeper meaning. In simile, one thing is like another, whereas in metaphor, one thing (speaking figuratively) is another. Here's a noteworthy example:

"Books are the mirrors of the soul." ~Virginia Woolf

If this metaphor were written as a simile, it might read something like this: "Books are like mirrors for the soul." That's still punchy, but suggesting that books are not *like* mirrors–they *are* mirrors–lends a certain intensity to the comparison. This is what makes metaphors so powerful in writing.

Despite their differences, when practicing writing metaphor, similes can provide a good starting point. Here's a creativity exercise to help you do just that:

First, take a simile, such as:

    Her smile was like the sun.

    He was as angry as a bear.

    Their excuses were like pebbles falling down a well.

Now, trim out the parts that make them similes, and you get:

    Her smile was ~~like~~ the sun.

    He was ~~as angry as a bear~~ an angry bear.

    Their excuses were ~~like~~ pebbles falling down a well.

Fluff them up a bit and give them a little polish, for poesy's sake:

>Her smile lit up the world around her.
>
>When angry, he became a bear.
>
>Their excuses were pebbles plunging down a bottomless well.

Context should inform how literally the reader should take these images.

What other comparisons might you draw between objects, actions, or ideas—ravens and writing desks, perhaps? Scribble up a few similes and see if you can metaphorize them!

_____
_____
_____
_____
_____
_____

"We may be small, but our hearts are large . . . metaphorically speaking." ~Octavius, *Night at the Museum*

Still Life

A visual artist can get inspiration from commonplace objects and create a whole masterpiece from what they see. And so can you. Without deliberating, pick a random object in the room you're sitting in and give it its own story.

- Where was it "born"?
- How did it come to be sitting in your room?
- Is it odd or does it blend into its environment?
- What's its life purpose?
- How does it feel about itself?
- Where will it be 10 years from now?

Can't Write It? Outline It!

Some people balk at the idea of creating an outline, but an outline is not written in stone. Its purpose is to keep you on target and moving forward by providing you with clear guideposts. It also gives you the opportunity to jump ahead if you're not a linear writer and work on a part you feel motivated to write. (Yes, it's okay to skip around.)

If you're writing fiction, you may prefer to write the story and find out what happens as you go, but if you already have the basic story in your head, there's no reason not to get it down on paper. You can also use the outline creation process to develop your story idea and establish your plot and subplots.

With nonfiction, make a list of all the main topics/ideas you want to cover. (You can also write a detailed synopsis of the work you intend to write and identify your main topics that way.) Figure out the natural progression of the topics and then put them in order. These will likely be your main chapters. Number your main topics to create chapters. Now, within each main topic, create subcategories (key points of the main topic), ordering them in their natural progression. These will likely be your subheads.

Your outline will probably evolve as new ideas come to you, so keep revising until you have a solid map to follow with many places to visit as the mood strikes you.

Go ahead: Try creating a draft now. Outline away!

Don't Scramble, Unscramble

This "fallen phrase" puzzle, which gives your creative mind a little break, is actually easier than it looks. Fill in each column in the top grid with the letters that have "fallen" (out of order) into the column in the grid directly below it. In other words, the letters in each column belong in the column above it.

When you arrange the letters correctly in the columns and read the puzzle from left to right, you'll reveal a bit of levity courtesy of Oscar Wilde to carry back with you to your writing desk.

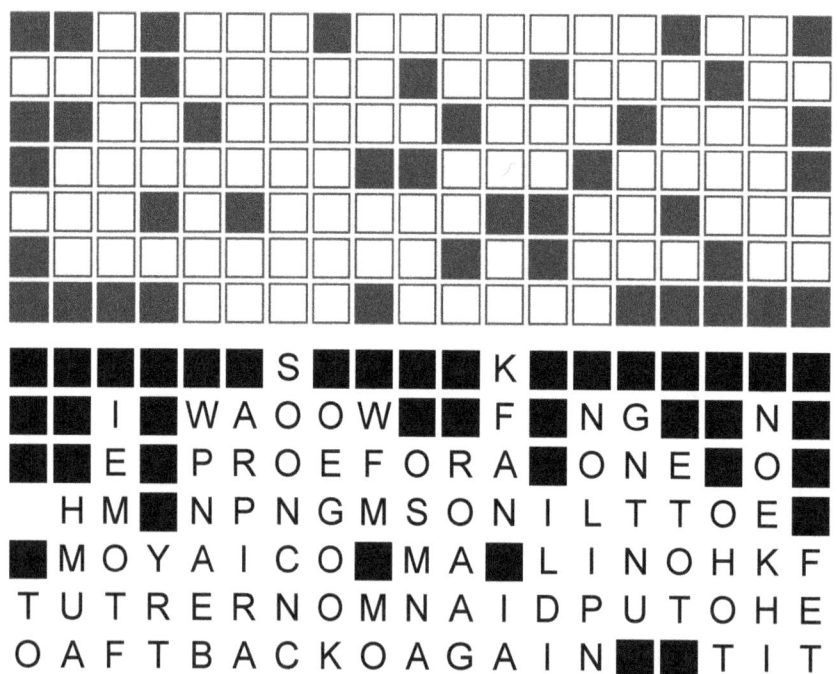

(The solution's on page 296.)

100

Get Another Writer's Perspective

A writing accountability partner is another writer who can be your sounding board and provide feedback as you navigate the writing process. Having a writer's perspective equips your partner to empathize with both the good and not-so-good experiences of the writing process, including Writer's Block.

Since a writer's time is valuable (as you know), you can be their writing accountability partner, too. This way you both benefit from the relationship. This person must be someone you trust as a fellow creative mind, so that when they offer you feedback or advice, you'll know they're giving it to you to improve your writing or motivate you, not to bog you down or to mold your writing to reflect what they subjectively think is best.

Create an agreement with your partner to check in with each other every few days and trade materials for another perspective at least twice a month. Choose a target word count and aim to share that number of words every two weeks.

It takes about an average of 20 minutes to read 5,000 words for pleasure, and even though you'll want to read at a slower pace to be able to provide thoughtful feedback, this isn't too much to expect of each other a few times a month.

My writing partner is: _____

Phone number(s): _____

E-mail address: _____

Map Out Your Brain

Have you ever planned a perfect day only for crummy weather to ruin it? The same thing can happen to your writing mojo when you've got a storm of stuff going on in your head. Luckily, unlike the weather outside right now, the weather in your mind is something you can take control of.

1. Spend a minute looking at the blank brain map. Notice some of the spaces are bigger than others and some are further in the back of the brain.

2. Hold this image in your mind. Close your eyes and ponder which thoughts, worries, and ideas might fill which spaces.

3. Open your eyes and fill in the "before" map.

4. Once you've mapped what's currently in your brain, close your eyes again and ponder the thoughts, ideas, and so on that you'd *like* your head to be full of.

5. Open your eyes and fill in the "after" map. When you're done, guide your brain to focus on your preferred thoughts and ideas.

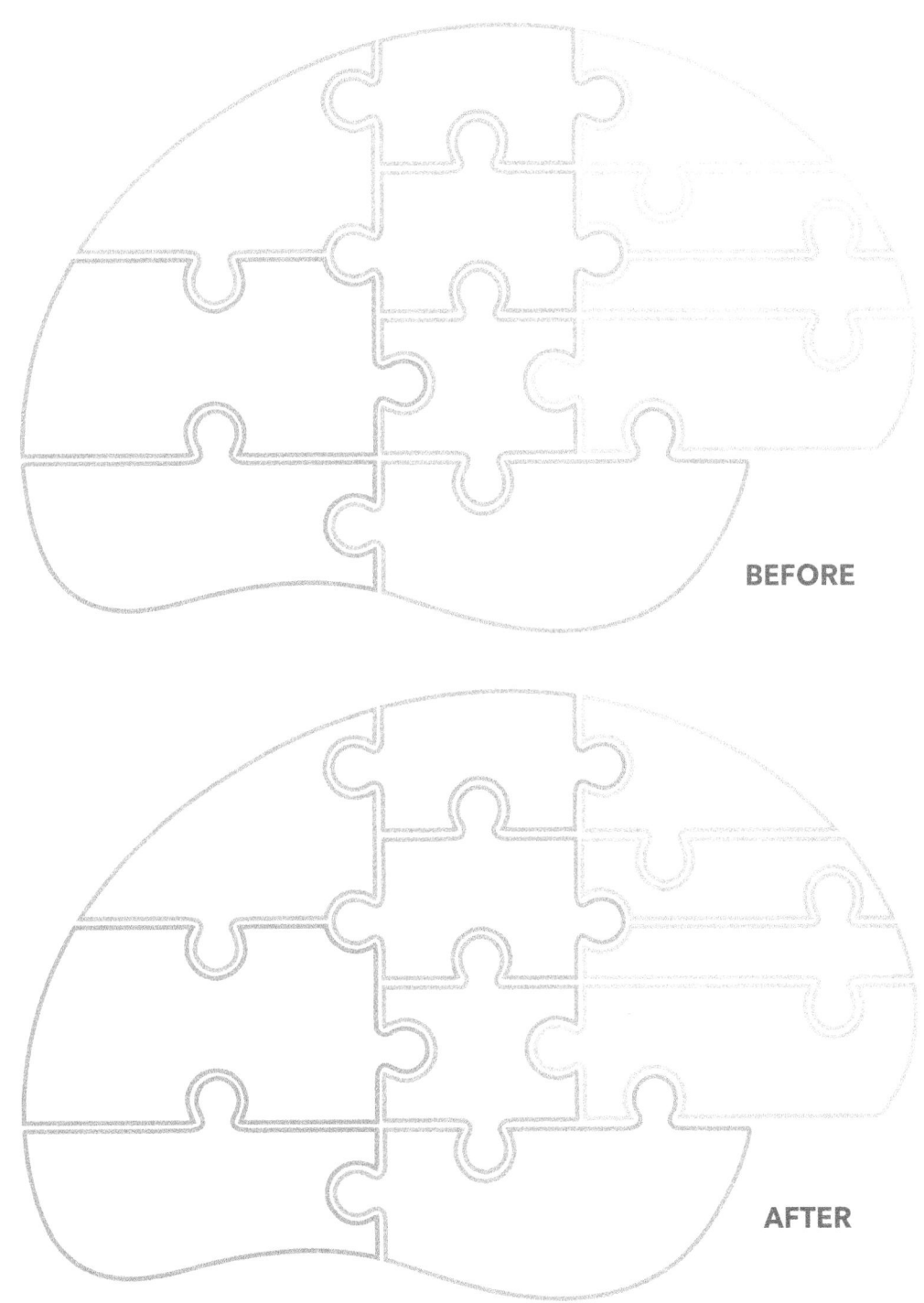

No Time to Panic!

Did you know that the word "panic" comes from the name of the Greek god Pan, who, among his other noteworthy traits, caused humans to flee in fear? Yes, at the root of panic is fear—fear that something is going to go very wrong and we must escape it.

But writing is not a life-or-death situation, and Writer's Block is definitely not a sabertooth who wants to make you this week's meal. So, put the task in perspective. What's the worst that could happen? You write nothing. But nobody's going to die because of it, not even you. So, next time you might feel the Greek god Pan at work, try one of the calming tips offered to find your courage to face the blank page.

Keep in mind that panic attacks and panic disorder aren't the same thing as run-of-the-mill, oh-my-god-I-haven't-written-a-word type of panic. It's probably a good idea to consult a professional if your type of panic is more serious than that.

10 QUICK CALMING TIPS

If you feel panicky as soon as you sit down to write, spend at least 5 minutes on one or more of the following before you put your fingers back on the keyboard:

1. Close your eyes and take a few deep breaths.
2. Listen to your favorite song.
3. Notice and name the sights, smells, and sounds around you.
4. Stand up and do the Hokey Pokey. Not kidding.
5. Drink a glass of water. Feel the liquid moving down your throat.
6. Gently stretch your neck and roll your shoulders.
7. Visualize yourself in a relaxed setting like a beach, forest, or lakeside.
8. Light incense or diffuse a relaxing essential oil.
9. Gently tense and release your muscle groups one at a time, starting with your toes.
10. Drink a cup of chamomile tea.

Remember the "Basics"

Ever get in the "writing zone," and suddenly, hours upon hours pass before you realize you've had nothing to eat or drink? Or before you realize you're getting a crick in your neck or stiff fingers and knees? Or before you realize you haven't even changed out of your pajamas?

Being in the zone can feel great in the moment, but if you're not taking care of your basic needs because you are so driven to write, you may fall into a Writer's Block slump where your brain and body say, "Enough already! We quit!" You're left longing for the zone, and no matter what you do, you can't get back there. That's a sign that it's time to recharge, but it's also time to plan for your next zone.

- Take a shower before sitting down to write, and wear comfortable clothing.
- Drape a sweater over the back of your chair in case you get chilly.
- Keep healthy snacks within reach while you're writing.
- Have a bottle or pitcher of water on your desk so that you are reminded to stay hydrated.
- Set an alarm to go off from time to time to remind you to stand up and stretch.

Yes, a long writing session where you completely immerse yourself in the project can feel amazing, but the aftermath might have a longer-lasting, creativity-depleting effect. So make sure your basic needs are taken care of during those highly creative writing sessions to keep Writer's Block at bay.

Brainstorm a plan to take care of the basics:

Writer's Nook

Just like a plant needs healthy soil, water, and plenty of sunshine to thrive, your mind needs the right environment to tap into its creative potential. Cultivating a writing environment that is always there for you allows you to keep that momentum that drives you to put fingers to keyboard in the first place.

A writing environment might be a desk in the corner of your home or your home office. It could also simply be your trusty laptop that you take with you to a coffee shop, the library, your bed, the park, and wherever else you feel inspired to write.

With that said, if you don't have a space in your home dedicated to writing, you can use your Writer's Block as an opportunity to set yourself up for future success by identifying a go-to area. When you have a dedicated space, simply going into that area can prompt your brain to prepare for a writing session, and then half the battle is won.

Here are a few things you might want to include in your nook:

- A computer or laptop with updated word-processing software
- A comfortable, ergonomic chair or backrest
- A desk or portable lap desk
- Headphones to block out unwanted noise
- A notepad or tablet to jot down ideas
- A good writing utensil (and a backup)
- A virtual or physical corkboard to pin up ideas and inspiration

Falling Down the Rabbit Hole

Summon your inner Alice and imagine that you fall down that rabbit hole over there into an entirely different universe. What would that universe look like? Write down every detail that springs to mind—the color of the sky, the sounds around you, the smells in the air, and everything in between. Remember, it's your alternate universe; the rules of this universe need not apply.

Time Yourself

Setting a timer for your writing sessions might provide you with enough external motivation to focus on the task of writing and keep you from falling down the rabbit hole of distractions.

There's only one rule: Do whatever you need to do to prepare, but once that timer starts, you must write.

So, let's say your usual writing session is from 10:00 a.m. to 12:00 p.m. It might seem reasonable to set the timer for two hours, but think about this: What else might happen during those two hours: a bathroom break, a coffee reheat, a smartphone notification, a dog who's barking at the front door, a little smackerel of something to appease a hunger rumble, a delivery notification from your Alexa . . . ?

So, instead of going for the whole hog, set your timer at 15-minute intervals. During those 15 minutes, nothing else matters short of an emergency.

When the timer goes off, if you're on an intense creative streak, keep writing; there's no reason to stop. If that's not the case, check in with yourself. Is there something you must do? If so, do it, and do it quickly. Aim to get back to your desk in 5 minutes or less, and then set your timer for the next 15 minutes.

Proceed this way throughout your writing session. If you find that timing yourself makes your more productive, keep at it. Eventually, you may want to set your timer for 30- or 45-minute intervals.

Try it now. Set your timer for 5 minutes and write whatever comes to your mind until your timer goes off. Keep your pen or pencil on the page the whole time. Timer set? Go!

A Picture Is Worth a Thousand Words

One photograph can tell a whole story in a single frame, which makes them so useful to the writer in search of words.

Let's say you're coming up short on description, and as much you want to write that ballroom scene, you've never actually stepped foot in a ballroom and your mind is drawing a blank.

Google "ballroom" and search through the images until you find one that resonates. Describe everything about the ballroom it in a bulleted-list format. Once you know that ballroom inside and out, it will be easier to work a few of those descriptors into your scene and build your setting.

This method can work for any scene your mind is having trouble imagining. You can get to know people this way, too. Need to put some dancers in that ballroom? Google "people dancing in a ballroom" or "ballroom dancers" next.

But that's not the only way to use photographs with regard to writing. You can search for images on any virtually topic to give yourself a better feel for the personal struggles or successes associated with that topic.

For practice, choose a place you've never visited and Google associated images. Look "inside" and "outside." Create your bulleted list of descriptors on the facing page and then write a paragraph describing your experience there in a new word document or on one of the blanks in the back.

A Journaling Sensation

Some writers are journalers and some journalers are writers, but not all journalers are writers in the sense we're talking about now. Logic problems aside, if you're a writer, chances are you also journal.

A journal is just a more sophisticated way to say diary—a "secret" place to write all about yourself, your feelings, and your experiences in life in a reflective sort of way. While some people publish their diaries, they are usually of a very personal, roughly written, sometimes rambling nature.

With your Writer's Block in mind, pull out your journal and read some of your entries. See if there's something in there that sparks an idea you can run with, build upon, and polish.

Don't keep a journal? Start one now. If you don't feel like you can write anything worth reading, write something that's not meant to be read by anyone but you.

"I never travel without my diary. One should always have something sensational to read in the train." ~Oscar Wilde

Cinematic Inspiration

"The book was better!"—Yeah, yeah, yeah, I know. But sometimes watching a film in your target *book* genre can help you get your writing mojo back!

Make a list of movies in your genre you think might get your juices flowing. Choose films you haven't seen in a long time or that you've never seen, as the twists you're not expecting might trigger that errant muse to come up with some twists of its own.

If you're writing nonfiction, think documentaries and YouTube videos on your topic. Branch out to TV series if your genre allows for it. Just be sure not to get sucked into binge-watching instead of writing! You could also look for films or series based on books, so you'll have new literary inspiration sources if the need arises.

_____   _____

_____   _____

_____   _____

_____   _____

_____   _____

Movies not doing it for your muse? See if any of those films are based on books! (Heck, if you find a film particularly inspiring, consider finding its textual origin anyways, since films tend to deviate notoriously from the books they're based on.)

"I discovered that rejections are not altogether a bad thing. They teach a writer to rely on his own judgment and to say in his heart of hearts, 'To hell with you.'" ~Saul Bellow

Fear Factor: Rejection

Is a fear of being rejected at the heart of your Writer's Block? This is different from the actual experience of rejection, which is an uncomfortable situation that brings up all sorts of unpleasant emotions that need to be worked through and potentially learned from. For now, let's just talk about the fear that it *might* happen.

Whose rejection do you fear? (Some writers might fear the industry, others their family and friends, maybe both.)

If you are rejected, what's the worst that could happen?

What feelings will it bring up for you?

What can you do to work through those feelings?

If the worst happened, what will you do to move forward and improve the situation?

Looking at the worst possible outcome and having a plan to move ahead can help put your fear in perspective and remind you that the power to move forward, in spite of rejection, is in your fingertips.

"You can please some of the people all of the time, you can please all of the people some of the time, but you can't please all of the people all of the time." ~John Lydgate

Facing Actual Rejection

Does anybody actually like rejection? It can be upsetting, discouraging, and even embarrassing. Whether you've just experienced your first rejection or your rejections are piling up and you feel that all your writing efforts are for naught, take heart in the fact that rejection is part of the biz. Many noteworthy authors were rejected by numerous publishers before they found that one publisher who took a chance on them.

Everyone has preferences—just remember that preferences are usually based on subjective opinion, not objective fact. There's always going to be someone who doesn't like what you write. In most cases, you're not writing for *that* person anyway—you're writing for the people who *will* like what you write. Nevertheless, if you're rejected by a publisher or agent, it can cut deeply. However, if they've taken time to tell you *why* you've been rejected, you can transmute their professional but subjective opinion into something more constructive with a little mental alchemy.

Remind yourself that people who take the time to give you critical feedback aren't rejecting *you*; they're trying to help you. If you're consistently being given similar reasons why someone is passing on your article or manuscript, consider talking to a professional editor about how to strengthen your work.

Nighty-Night

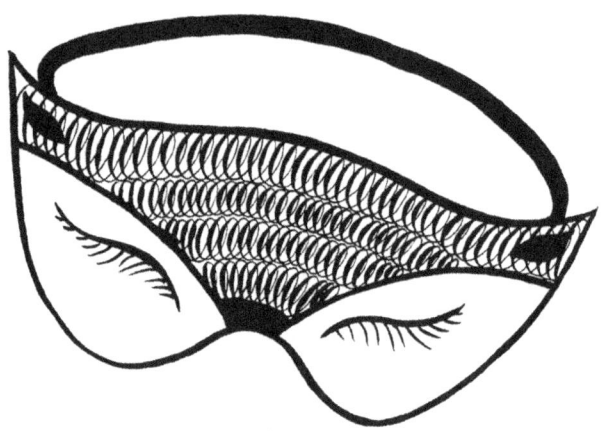

Everyone has a bad night's sleep sometimes. Maybe the room was too warm or too cold, or you had too much coffee, or you slept in too late yesterday morning or went to bed too late last night. If it's any of these, a bedtime routine and a sleep schedule can be helpful.

In fact, getting restful and regular sleep is one of the most basic ways to take care of your physical and mental health—and you need both to write well. So, if a lack of good sleep is making it difficult to write, give this simple routine a try:

- Choose a bedtime and a wake-up time. If you have to get up at, say, 7 AM, plan to be in bed and ready to go to sleep at least 8 hours before that. So 11 PM. Sounds doable, yeah? Then set an alarm for your wake-up time.

- Put your tech to bed first. At least an hour before bedtime, shut off the TV, plug in your phone, and power down the computer or tablet—unplug the microwave if you have to!

- If a warm bath helps you unwind, try that. Add all the bubbles you want and use your favorite soap. Read a good book, listen to music, doodle, knit—whatever chills you out, take the time to do it. You might even—dare I say it?—write a little something.

- When you wake up, get up. Don't hit snooze. Waking up at the same time every day should help you sleep better at night. Plus, getting right out of bed can feel pretty successful on its own!

> ▶ **TIP:** If you know your poor sleep is less about what's in your coffee cup and more about what's in your mind, try this: Before you turn in tonight, write a brief description of what's nagging at you and what you can do about the situation. Then sleep on it.

"It is a common experience that a problem difficult at night is resolved in the morning after the committee of sleep has worked on it." ~John Steinbeck

"Learn the rules like a pro, so you can break them like an artist." ~Pablo Picasso

So Many Rules, So Little Written

As a writer, it's certainly helpful to know the basic rules of grammar, but if you start stressing over every comma, fragment, dangling participle, and run-on while you are working on your first draft, your creativity can take a nosedive—especially if you find all the rules daunting—and then Writer's Block comes rearing its annoying head.

So, forget about the mechanics—for now. Write as well as you can without thinking about the rules. Don't rely on software as the final say, but you can always run a grammar and spell check later. Plus, you're not expecting that first draft to be polished anyway. You'll have a chance to smooth out the writing when you begin your revisions.

> Consider taking a grammar course. It doesn't hurt to know and practice the rules of grammar if you're a writer. If you choose to ignore a certain grammar rule because it conflicts with your writing style, at least you *know* that you're ignoring it—and you can take it up with your editor.

"As for writer's block, I regard it as my unconscious mind telling me that I'm making a gross mistake in the project I'm working on. It's not a problem, it's a blessing, and the mystery is to find out the mistake, toss out the ineffective section, and write a new version that works." ~Orson Scott Card

Reinvent

Let's take a lesson here from award-winning author Orson Scott Card and consider for a moment that your Writer's Block is serving an important purpose: It's telling you that something you've written doesn't jibe with your vision for the completed work.

No one wants to get so stuck in rewrites that there's no progress, but going back over what you've written is sometimes necessary to find your way around the block and move forward.

For instance, if there's a scene or chapter in an earlier part of your work that's weakening the whole chain, copy it over to a new file and reinvent it from a different, more in-depth perspective. Perhaps there's a dangling plot point you can omit or a character who needs to be "killed," or maybe you've introduced a concept that needs further explanation or even an explanatory illustration like a graph or chart.

Look at your reinventions as part of the writing process. You may feel like you're going backward, but really what you're doing is finding a new direction that will eventually get you to your end goal more quickly.

How do you feel about reinventing?

_____

_____

_____

_____

Lighten Your Stress Load

What's stressing you out that might be interfering with your ability to have a good writing session? Maybe it's housekeeping stuff; maybe it's world events. List your top-10 stressors on the facing page.

Review each item on your list. Is it something you can control? If not, cross it out. It will probably work itself out whether or not you stress about it, so why worry?

If it is something you can change, jot down a possible solution. For instance: Mail piling up? The solution is to sort it. Bathroom a mess? Clean it. Bills going up? Create or revise a budget. Roped into something you don't want to do? Say no. On the outs with a friend? Call them.

Now, review your list again and identify the ones that would take under an hour to resolve. Do one of them, and then start your writing session. Afterward or maybe tomorrow, choose another quickie from your list. Cross off each remaining stressor as you resolve it.

Sure, there will be some things you can't cross off today or even this week or even this year. Just chip away at those things a little at a time the same way you're doing with your Writer's Block.

1. _____
2. _____
3. _____
4. _____
5. _____
6. _____
7. _____
8. _____
9. _____
10. _____

"You can do anything—but not everything." ~David Allen

Good Morning, Sunshine!

You may be so used to rolling out of bed and into your computer chair that you might not go outside until the mail comes—if you even go outside at all on your writing days.

Instead, get a few minutes of sunlight first thing in the morning to get your day started on the right foot.

1. Open your door, step outside, close your eyes, and let the sunlight wash your face.

2. Spend a moment visualizing a writing goal you want to complete today—or just see yourself full of energy with the words flowing easily from your fingers onto the page.

3. Now, go about your day recharged.

Screening for Problems

- Maybe your eyes are glued to the wrong screen. Try downloading a word-processing app, like Google Docs, to your tablet or phone and see if your brain focuses better on a smaller screen.

- Delete social media apps for a little while to cut down on distractions.

- Change your word-processor background color. Maybe making the background, or even the virtual page, a different color will give your eyes a much-needed change of scenery.

- Switch the font. Maybe you normally type in **Times New Roman** (a serif font) but **Arial** (a sanserif font) would be a welcome change. Some writers swear that **Comic Sans**—yes, *that* **Comic Sans**—has made a huge difference in their productivity. (Just don't submit it to anyone like that.)

- Increase or decrease the point size of your typeface or zoom in or out to make your words larger or smaller.

- Try single-spaced or double-spaced paragraphs.

- Change your medium. Do you usually type in MS Word? Try Pages or Google Docs. Or write on paper! Pick up a spiral-bound notebook and see if writing "the old-fashioned way" gets your juices flowing.

"I don't know where my ideas come from. I will admit, however, that one key ingredient is caffeine. I get a couple cups of coffee into me and weird things just start to happen."
~Gary Larson, *The Far Side*

Cuppa Joe

Do you rely on caffeine in the morning and perhaps throughout the day to keep your brain awake? No judgment here. The famous French writer Voltaire supposedly drank a lot of the stuff and one of his doctors warned him it would be the death of him. He lived to be 83, which in 1778 was pretty impressive.

We hear a lot of negative stuff about coffee these days to the point where we may struggle to avoid it. For some coffee drinkers, this can feel like slow torture. Go ahead and make yourself a fresh pot if a wave of sluggishness is keeping you from writing. But if there's a valid reason for you to limit your intake of caffeine, try a cup of invigorating herbal tea instead.

Cracking Under Pressure?

Unless you're facing an actual deadline from work, school, or your publisher, most forms of pressure to write are internal. But let's talk about those external pressures when you absolutely *must* meet a deadline.

Some people work best under pressure and may even produce their best writing when someone's breathing down their neck, but that's not true for all writers. If the pressure is too much, take these steps:

1. Remind yourself that *you* are in control of your actions.

2. Figure out how much you have to write (word count) and how long you have. Create a realistic writing schedule (see page 74).

3. Organize the writing task into step-by-step action items. For example:

a) get clear on the topic

b) gather research

c) brainstorm ideas

d) create an outline

e) write first draft

f) revise

g) proofread

h) finalize

Then tackle each step one at a time.

4. Ask for help if you need it to complete it. For instance, ask one of your colleagues or a classmate to assist you or hook up with an editor.

Now, if someone's nagging you to write without a looming deadline, take that as a compliment. They're looking forward to reading what you're working on. Other than that, don't pay them any attention. Rushing your writing to please others can put a dent in your passion and commitment.

Think about what you'd like to say to them the next time they ask you, "Hey, when are you going to be finished writing that?" even if it's, "I'm just not sure. I'll let you know when it's done."

Get Off Your Own Back

Putting pressure on yourself to write is not a negative thing in and of itself, but if it's freezing up your fingers and messing with your mind, it's time to take a step back and figure out *why* you are pressuring yourself—and if it's really worth it.

- ☐ Are you trying to prove yourself to others?
- ☐ Are you tired of what you're writing and you just want to "get it done" already?
- ☐ Do you need to make money and hope you can produce a bestseller in record time or get another article published before the rent comes due?
- ☐ Do you feel like you *should* be writing because you're good at it, not because you're passionate about it?

Rushing your writing to prove yourself to others or "just get it done" can suck the joy out of the writing process. And telling yourself you *should* do something even though you don't want to probably isn't going to get you where you want to be. If you make your money as a writer, that's another story entirely. Pressuring yourself is good, but don't forget to reward yourself with breaks.

Whatever the case, if you put too much pressure on yourself to produce, you may end up hating writing, which, as a writer, is the last thing you want to do. So cut yourself some slack from time to time.

It's a Little Puzzling

This "fallen phrase" puzzle, which gives your creative mind a little break, is actually easier than it looks. Fill in each column in the top grid with the letters that have "fallen" (out of order) into the column in the grid directly below it. In other words, the letters in each column belong in the column above it.

Arrange the letters correctly and read the grid from left to right to reveal a bit of humor, courtesy of Groucho Marx, to lighten the Writer's Block stress that's been dogging you.

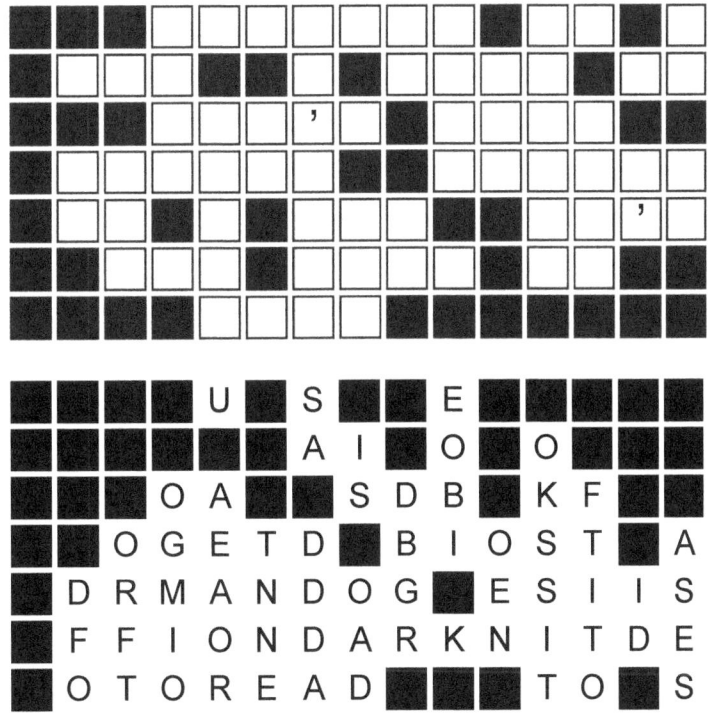

(The solution's on page 296.)

Get in the Mood

If you're not in the mood to write today, then what *are* you in the mood to do? If you can, do it. You may not be able to hop a flight to the Caribbean on a whim, but maybe checking out a local park or museum you've been meaning to visit will be enough of a change of scenery (and bonus: a source of inspiration). Maybe you've been meaning to learn a new hobby. Hit the local craft store and give it a try.

List the things you'd like to do instead of writing. You can use this as a go-to list of things to do when your muse goes AWOL.

"Write it. Shoot it. Publish it. Crochet it, sauté it, whatever. MAKE." ~Joss Whedon

Frozen in Fear

Is fear of failure causing your Writer's Block? Could be—after all, it's a common theme in literature and in life. But could you also be stuck because you are actually afraid to succeed? It can be terrifying to think that if you write something amazing, it will put a burden on you to always write amazing prose.

List five of your fears related to writing:

1. _____
2. _____
3. _____
4. _____
5. _____

Now ask yourself how likely those fears are to be realized. And, if they do come to pass, what's the worst that could happen? Looking at your fears this way can help you thaw out enough to move forward.

> "Don't let the fear of striking out hold you back." ~Babe Ruth

Declutter Your Space, Declutter Your Mind

Look around you. Could your environment be a contributing factor to your Writer's Block? Is your desk cluttered? Think of your desk as your mind. A cluttered mind is no place for work to get done, and neither is a cluttered desk. Clearing your desk can be as good for your writing process as clearing your mind is for your stress levels.

1. Make three piles (use boxes if there's a lot of clutter): keep, give away, and garbage. Sort out what's garbage first—dried-out pens, junk mail, expired coupons, etc. Now divide what remains into "keep" and "give away" piles.

2. Once you've decided what on your desk needs to stick around, further: Is there anything among this "keep" stuff that has nothing to do with writing? Pull it out and set it aside.

3. Now sort what remains into categories. Put pens with pens (check for duds as you go and add them to the garbage pile), paperclips with paperclips, important papers with—you get it. Now find a dedicated spot in, on, or near your desk for each of these sets of items to live.

4. Now deal with the non-writing stuff. (If you've been putting off dealing with what's on those important papers, by the way, now might be a good time to take care of them.) Put those non-writing things where they go and make a commitment NOT to put them back in your writing space. Box up mementos.

5. Finally, take that trash pile to the garbage or recycling bin and bask in the glow of your tidy new desk!

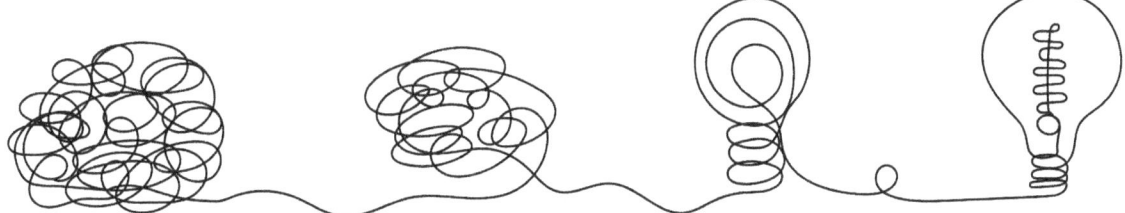

Reveal the Hidden Message

This is no ordinary word search. Once you find all the words in the word list, you'll find an important message just for you in the remaining letters. This is a bit of beast, but finishing it feels good (speaking from personal experience).

AUTHOR	DRAFT	PHRASE	REWRITE
AUTOBIOGRAPHY	ESSAY	POEM	SCRIBBLE
AUTOGRAPH	EXPRESS	PRINT	SCRIBE
BOOK	FICTION	RECAST	SIGN
CHARACTERS	FORMULATE	RECORD	SPEECH
COMPOSE	FRAME	REDRAFT	TRANSCRIBE
COMPOSITION	MANUSCRIPT	REGISTER	TYPE
CRAFT	MEMOIR	REVISE	WORDS
DESCRIBE	NONFICTION		

. . . .
Write the solution here:

___ ___ ___ ___ ___ ___ ___ ___ ___ ___ ___ ___ ___ ___

___ ___ ___ ___ ___ ___ ___ ___ ___ ___ ___ ___ ___ ___ ___ .

```
Y D O Y S C U S T F E C N A H
T E E H P N H F C S R O C P M
R S T P E R A A O R I A A U E
A C I A E R U P R T I R M X M
N R R R C T M W I A G B P E O
S I W G H O S S O O C R B E I
C B E O C H O Y T R E T P L R
R E R I O P U U R S D Y E B E
I P L B M Y A S S E T S B R E
B O O O C E T A L U M R O F S
E E C T N O I T C I F N O N A
K M N U R E G I S T E R K O R
W T F A R D E R E C A S T N H
T P I R C S U N A M T N I R P
D R O C E R E V I S E S I G N
```

The Naughty List

What's something you've always wanted to write, but you haven't because you think you "can't" or "shouldn't"? Can't read music but you want to write a musical? Want to write a psychological thriller but worry you'll freak out the lady in HR? How about a steamy romance your mom might cringe to know you're writing?

Make a "naughty list" of three things you've always wanted to write but never had the courage to try. Then pick one of them and brainstorm the idea on the facing page. Forget all the "what would my neighbors think?" concerns and write uninhibited!

1. _____
2. _____
3. _____

Remember this: We writers write first and foremost for ourselves. An audience of one (yourself) is audience enough to justify writing what you like to write. If you have fun brainstorming this idea, consider exploring the project further!

"A writer is someone who has taught his mind to misbehave." ~Oscar Wilde

8 Tree Lessons

Trees begin as tiny, fragile seeds. But with enough water, nourishment, and sunlight, they become thriving and resilient beings. The same can be true of your writing process, so take a few more lessons from the trees.

1. Take your time growing as a writer. There's no need to rush the process of honing your craft.

2. Create a solid foundation for your work, including research, lessons, practice, and commitment.

3. Stay flexible and adaptable. If you are too rigid in your process, you are more likely to snap.

4. Let ideas that have outlived their usefulness fall away.

5. Embrace the seasons of your life and know that different "weather" might call for a change in behavior.

6. Put out feelers in many different places, and reach for the stars from a stable base.

7. Think of feedback as nutrients to help you grow as a writer.

8. Nourish yourself on the fruits of your labor.

Reflect on these lessons as you color in the tree on the facing page.

Hack Your Brain

The interesting thing about the mind is it cannot tell the difference between what's real and what isn't. It only knows what it sees—whether it's physical or imagined. So, find a comfortable seat in a room outside of your writer's nook. Spend 5 minutes visualizing the following scenario as vividly and with as much detail as possible:

1. Imagine yourself walking into your writing space. You sit down, feeling inspired and motivated to write. Your mind is bubbling with creative juices.

2. You open a new word-processing document and see the cursor flashing. You place your fingers on the keyboard and notice how smooth they feel, how ready they are for your touch.

3. Your fingers start flying across the keyboard, word after word, sentence after sentence, paragraph after paragraph. You don't need to see what it says. Just visualize the pages filling with invigorating prose.

4. Feel the joy and pride in your work as your word count increases.

5. Save and close the document. Bask in that sense of accomplishment.

Did that? Good. Now do it again, but this time in real life.

Script It

Along the lines of the visualization exercise on the facing page, you may find that actually writing a script for your ideal writing scenario brings this even more to life for you . . . and that much closer to reality. Use the previous steps as writing prompts and write your script here:

Decorate Your Writing Space

Having a go-to spot to write can be helpful for putting yourself in the headspace to write, but it's not enough to just huddle in a nondescript corner. Making that designated space *your* space can be a big boost to your muse, especially in times of literary drought.

1. Make a list of things you enjoy. Focus on items or activities that evoke feelings of happiness, security, confidence, and so on.

2. Find a place in your home to utilize as "your space"—whether that be an office, closet, patio, or even kitchen table (when you aren't using it for eating, of course). The important thing is to have a place that will also carry limited distractions because the last thing you would want is to be brought out of the zone or "accidentally" waste a few hours on your phone.

3. Finally, the fun part: decoration! Remember that list you created? Create or purchase a few items from that list to decorate your space with. Just like it is important to surround yourself with good, loving people, the same could be said for the physical items you keep around the house. In the case of your writing space, emphasize items that make you happy, evoke good memories, and make you feel confident and productive.

Flawless Figment

perfection (n) 1 : the quality or state of being perfect: such as : freedom from fault or defect : FLAWLESSNESS

That's *Merriam-Webster's* first definition of "perfection."

Think about your favorite book. I'll bet if you dig deep enough, you'll find at least one thing you might consider less than perfect. A plot point, character detail, descriptive copy, random typo, the book cover—whatever.

Now consider that that one thing you don't love might be someone else's favorite detail (well, not the typo). Here's the rub: Neither you nor that hypothetical other person are wrong.

Art is subjective. Writing is art. Just like some people don't dig Salvador Dalí's paintings, some people may not dig your writing. But Dalí's work is worth millions, and there may be tons of people out there who think your work is million-dollar reading.

"Have no fear of perfection—you'll never reach it." ~Salvador Dalí

Breathe, Write

Do you hold your breath when you're stressed? How about when you're writing? Do you sit slumped in your chair, compressing your torso so there's less room for your lungs to fill with air and you can't take a deep breath?

A relaxed mind is more likely to produce words than one that's uptight—and the best way to relax is to breathe. Sure, it's one of those things that ordinarily happens on its own (thank goodness), but when done consciously and deeply, it can help move you from a state of frustration into a more receptive mood.

When you have a moment, check out some breathing exercises online and practice them. For now, just sit up (stop scrunching those abs), and take a deep breath in through your nose and let it out through your mouth.

As you breathe in, feel the air expand your lungs and belly, and when you release it, feel your belly and lungs deflate.

Do this consciously a couple of times during your writing sessions to stay relaxed and receptive to your creativity.

And, as you color in the image alongside this page, pay attention to your breath the whole time. When you're feeling more relaxed, get back to writing!

A Matter of Opinion

To get yourself used to the perfectly acceptable idea of imperfection, think of something you might consider perfect just the way it is, like the ideal slice of pizza. It's the consummate combination of cheese, sauce, and just-right crusty bread—to you.

Now, try to see this from the perspective of someone who dislikes this slice of pizza or whatever else you thought of, and ask yourself why they might feel that way. For example, maybe the gooey cheese grosses them out because they're vegan or the doughy bread is no good for their gluten sensitivity. Maybe they just don't like the combo of bread, cheese, and tomato sauce. Maybe they had a bad experience with tomatoes. Maybe they like less cheese. Maybe the perfect slice to them has pepperoni, too. Who knows?

Now think of your writing as this ideal slice of pizza. Clearly, it's not for everyone. Perfection is totally subjective. Everyone brings their own experience to the opinions they formulate. What's perfect to someone may be trash to another—and anywhere in between.

For each slice of the pizza pie on the right, fill it with a quality you personally admire to include in your recipe for a tasty piece of writing.

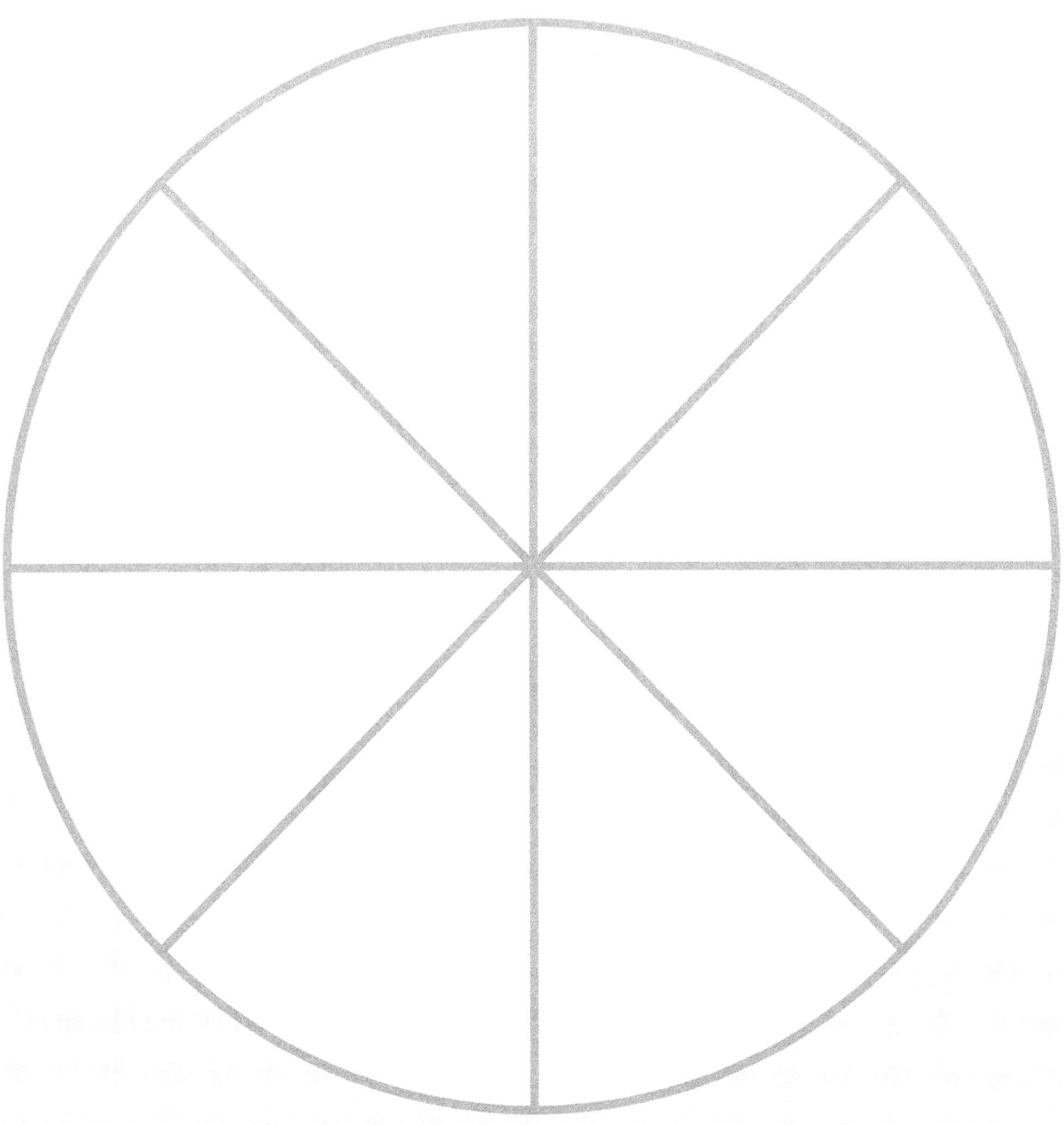

"Do I Suck at This?"

If you stare at any word long enough, it'll start to look silly. It's the same with your writing. One day you might read something you wrote and say, "Wow! This is *really* good!" A week later, you might think it sucks with no hope of improving. Somewhere between the two—thinking it's *really* good and thinking it *totally* sucks—is likely where you'll find the truth. It's good and can get better.

However, if you have to sincerely ask if you suck at something, chances are there's room for improvement. This isn't about having read and revised your work so many times that everything starts to read a little wonky. That's simply a sign that it's time to step away from it so you can see it with a fresh perspective at another time. Rather, this is about knowing deep down that you need to put more time into honing your writing skills. Remember, all writing is editable. A blank page isn't.

> "I hereby grant you permission to write crap. The more the better. Remember, crap makes the best fertilizer." ~Pat Pattison

No Compromises

Are you trying to squeeze in your writing time at random hours on random days around your *must-dos* and wondering why you're coming up short? Is it possible that you just haven't made a serious commitment to write by realistically scheduling it into your life?

To get started, figure out what you *absolutely cannot* compromise—a day job, a full class schedule, caring for kids and/or animal friends, family time, exercise, grocery shopping, preparing meals, etc.? Write down all the things you simply cannot get out of doing:

_____   _____

_____   _____

_____   _____

Now, pencil all those commitments into a weekly planner and block out time for their usual duration. What's left? That's your available time to write. Block off time for a writing session each day, even if you can only scrape up a half hour on some days. Block off longer sessions on the days when you have a little more leeway.

Treat this time like you'd treat your other serious commitments—because it *is* a serious commitment. Once you've written it on your calendar along with all your other "absolutely cannot compromise" things, your writing time carries the same weight. Short of a major life event, this time is to be solely dedicated to writing.

> ▶ **TIP:** If your life schedule starts to shift, don't forget to reevaluate your weekly planner and reschedule your writing sessions.

Busting Stress

Are you navigating some rough waters in your life that have nothing to do with your writer's life? Your stress level might be so high that the thought of writing is just a fleeting fantasy. But you *want* to write or you wouldn't be reading this right now. So, what's a writer to do? Try to get a handle on your stress. First of all, acknowledge that you are stressed so that you can begin the process of relieving it and get back into your groove.

- **Ask for help.** If you are so overloaded that you can hardly take a moment to yourself, talk to people who care about you and brainstorm some ways to alleviate a few of your burdens. Who you gonna call? Write their names here:

  _____, _____, _____

- **Don't forget to breathe.** You may feel like you can't control much during this time, but one thing you can always control is your breath. Set an intermittent reminder on your phone to stop and breathe throughout the day. Do it right now. Find an app that chimes at intervals.

- **Do the next best thing.** You can't do everything at once, so focus on just the next thing that needs to get done. Multitasking when you're super stressed can lead to mistakes because you aren't giving a task your full attention.

- **Journal your thoughts before you go to bed.** Okay, so you're not able to write for others right now, so just write for yourself. Even if it's just for 5 minutes before lights out. Who knows? This might end up being good fodder for your future writing project.

Too stressed to even write in a journal? Color this dove instead. Doves are a symbol of peace and serenity.

"Great things are not done by impulse, but by a series of small things brought together."
~Vincent Van Gogh

Orient Your GPS

Sometimes a writer starts writing without any idea where the words will take them. It's like walking through the woods looking for the street you know is out there, but you're in unfamiliar territory without a GPS and you're not sure what you'll encounter on your way.

That can be an exciting adventure or an aimless venture. After some time, you may find yourself wandering without purpose, so you plop down right where you are, hoping a friendly park ranger will find you and take you home. Getting lost in the woods is no fun. The same is true when you get lost in your manuscript and don't know how to move forward. You need direction.

- What was your starting point? Where does the introduction or chapter 1 begin?

- What is your end point? How does the last chapter resolve the story or conclude the discussion?

- What roads, side roads, and highways will take you where you want to go? What are the chapters between the beginning and the end?

- What landmarks will you pass? What are the major topics or plot points?

- What pitstops will you make? What are the subtopics or side stories?

Ask yourself these questions to reorient yourself toward your destination and take the next step to find your way out.

Cube It to Use It

Imagine your Writer's Block as a cube with six sides. Grab it out of your head and put it in front of you. (You'll need to ramp up your imagination for that part.) Now, think of the topic you want to write about. Each of the six sides of your Writer's Block represents a different perspective. This is generally known as "cubing."

Follow the sides of the cube in order and respond in writing to the prompts on the facing page. Don't waste time trying to sound good; this is simply an exercise to generate a more three-dimensional view of your topic, which might be the angle you need to start writing about it.

> **SIDE 1:** Describe your topic in as much detail as possible.
>
> **SIDE 2:** Compare your topic to a similar one. How is it the same? How does it differ?
>
> **SIDE 3:** Associate it with your relevant thoughts, feelings, and experiences.
>
> **SIDE 4:** Analyze it by breaking it down into its parts.
>
> **SIDE 5:** Apply your topic to real-life scenarios.
>
> **SIDE 6:** Argue both the pros and cons of your topic, considering strengths and weaknesses.

SIDE 1: _____

_____

_____

SIDE 2: _____

_____

_____

SIDE 3: _____

_____

_____

SIDE 4: _____

_____

_____

SIDE 5: _____

_____

_____

SIDE 6: _____

_____

_____

"Not all those who wander are lost." ~J.R.R. Tolkien, *The Fellowship of the Ring*

Find Your Way

Think of your Writer's Block as a maze . . . and find your way through it.

(The solution's on page 297.)

Wash That Block Away

Writer's Block can be a heavy weight to carry. And, as you know, if you carry any heavy weight around long enough, you'll start to sweat. Washing away the metaphorical sweat from lugging around your Writer's Block can unclog your pores and allow your creativity to flow freely again. Try this:

1. Turn on the shower and step in.

2. Visualize that your Writer's Block is grime on your skin.

3. Gently wash that grime away. Feel it rinsing off your skin and disappearing down the drain.

4. As you wash, feel yourself gaining a sense of clarity and purpose.

5. When all the grime has been washed away, imagine that stream of water pouring inspiration and ideas into your head. Feel them washing over you and soaking into your skin until you feel absolutely covered in wonderful, clean, fresh inspiration.

Uncover the Writing Advice

Cryptograms are a popular brain workout, and as you know, you want your brain to be sharp when you sit in front of your keyboard. A puzzle like this gives your brain a chance to problem-solve, which comes in handy when you're trying to work out that dangling plot point.

Each letter in the cryptogram stands for another letter. For example, A might be R or G might be T. It takes some guesswork and trial and error. Use the handy grid to keep track—and use a pencil with an eraser!

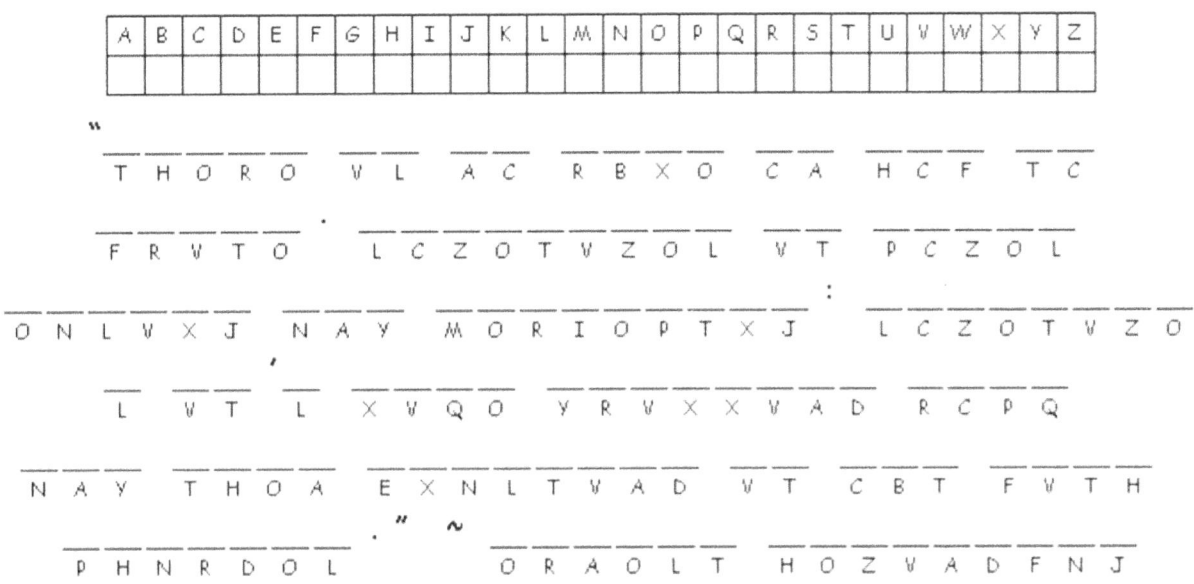

(The solution's on page 297.)

Not Tonight, Words, I Have a Headache

If you're so stressed about writing that it's actually making your head hurt, you and your work will likely both suffer if you continue. Honor your headache by doing something to alleviate it. Don't just try to power through, hoping it will go away.

Maybe that means putting a cool, damp cloth on your forehead, closing your eyes for a while, rubbing your temples, sniffing a refreshing essential oil, or turning the lights down or completely off. If you can, get some sleep. Chances are your brain needs a rest.

Word Count Bull's-eye

If you've been struggling to hit your target word count, you might find yourself tempted to "pad" the narrative a little. In doing so, you're not so much hitting your target word count as you are giving your readers (and yourself, when you eventually edit your work) more work to do.

Think of the vast area of space around the bull's-eye on a dart board. Getting a dart anywhere on a dartboard translates into points.

Try the dartboard method for your target word count. Set your bull's-eye—your peak target count—and then build backward in word-count increments from there. So if writing 1,000 words constitutes a bull's-eye day for you, set your minimum word count at 100, or 50, or even 10. Set increments from there every hundred words or so.

Maybe a target word count of 10 feels silly, but treating that minimum count like a goal in itself will keep you playing the game. Even if you don't hit the bull's-eye, you'll still be on the board!

You can even keep a log of how many words you've written each day so you can see your progress—and any amount of writing is progress—which can be a huge encouragement on those days when that bull's-eye is hard to hit.

"So the writer who breeds more words than he needs, is making a chore for the reader who reads." ~Dr. Seuss

Write a "Bad" Page

Set a timer for 15 minutes and make a commitment to write at least 250 words about one of the following topics. During the whole 15 minutes, just keep writing. Don't think too much about the words you use. Give yourself permission to write badly.

- A love relationship between a glass and the water inside that slowly gets sipped away.
- An argument between the ketchup and mustard on the refrigerator shelf.
- A doorway in an old house that thinks back on all those who have walked through it.
- A flower that blooms and withers in the same day.
- A coffee pot that brews in the morning and gets poured from throughout the day.
- A favorite pen that gets lost in the back of the drawer and misses its writer.

"You can always edit a bad page.
You can't edit a blank page."
~Jodi Picoult

Skip Around

Maybe it's not the whole writing project that's causing your Writer's Block, but the part of it that you're working on. If you're a "start from the beginning and write to the end" kind of person, you might struggle with the idea of hopping around. Maybe it makes you feel disorganized. But if your muse is really itching for a change of scenery, now might be the time to let it roam more freely.

- Try fleshing out or tweaking your outline. Maybe you've started with simple bullet points and you've never gotten around to filling in the gaps. Now's the time to try! You might find that some bullet points you weren't sure how to expand will become clearer as you fill in the rest.

- Say you're stuck on a particular chapter because your brain keeps jumping ahead to a key scene in your story or an important point you want to make. Open a new file or key in a page break and start that scene or write that message! (Make sure you label it for later.)

- Keep a file of "loose change" writing—bits of dialogue, pieces of description, and snippets of narrative you may or may not have a place for yet. Maybe these little gems aren't destined for the project(s) you're currently working on, but they could just be the seeds for a new story someday!

- Maybe you know how you want your story to end, but the middle is still a little murky in your mind. Try writing that ending! Perhaps a line of dialogue or an object you'll find yourself writing into the ending will trigger an idea to fill in the middle.

Once you've let your muse wander, come back to the place where you got stuck. If you still feel stuck in that spot, keep writing what you're *not* stuck on until you don't feel stuck anymore.

> "A story should have a beginning, a middle and an end, but not necessarily in that order."
> ~Jean-Luc Godard

Just Wanna Have Fun?

Everybody needs downtime, but words don't write themselves—unfortunately. So you'll have to make peace with the idea that you, as a writer, actually spend much of your "downtime" writing. What's more, a writer's life can often be a lonely one, especially if you have to forego social plans and other fun activities to stick to your writing commitment.

If you start resenting that commitment, however, you may very well find yourself up against Writer's Block. Of course you can and should take time to yourself, but often, writers need to need to actually schedule their downtime between writing sessions and projects.

Make plans for *after* your deadlines to let loose and celebrate with your friends (you know, those friends who call in the middle of a writing session to shoot the breeze).

Schedule in your fun the way you do your writing sessions. No schedule? See page 74.

"Impostor!"

One day you're feeling all gung ho about your work. What you've written amazes you. Wow! You knew you had it in you! You bask in the glow of what you've accomplished so far, and it feels great! *Mmmm.*

Then, suddenly, like someone flipped the switch, you start questioning your credibility. Who are you to write this? Do you even have the experience, the know-how, or the expertise? Yikes! You start feeling like a fraud, and you lose focus. Will readers find you out? Will they know you have no idea what you're doing?! Your way forward seems murky.

Feeling like an impostor can be a powerful obstacle in the way of moving forward with confidence. But your mind is just playing tricks on you. Remind yourself how far you've come. In the space below, list the evidence you've gathered to get back your original enthusiasm:

What personal or professional experience do you have with regard to your topic?

_____

_____

_____

What makes you uniquely qualified to write what you're writing?

_____

_____

_____

Other Authors as Inspiration

Comparison shopping yourself against your favorite author on social media can be discouraging, so consider hiding their feed for now—especially if you're still in the drafting stage. Drawing inspiration from successful authors is all well and good, but if it's discouraging you from even writing, give yourself a break.

With that said, there are some elements of other authors' work you can safely go to for inspiration. Try these ideas on for size:

- Pin some images of your favorite book covers on your vision pin-up board.
- Look for fan art of characters whose depth of development you'd love to emulate in your own character building.
- Flip through other authors' writing guides and/or take one of their online writing classes.
- Print out poignant lines from authors who inspire you and place them where you can see them as you write. In fact, find one now and write it here:

_____

_____

_____

▶ *Remember: The key here is to draw inspiration, not comparison.*

A Circuitous Route

The path forward isn't always so straightforward. Let your mind explore other avenues. When you reach the puzzle's center, you might be ready to write your first line.

(The solution's on page 298.)

Who Wrote It?

A well-known and often much-loved author wrote each of the books that comprise the clues for this crossword. Yeah, that's a lot of names to know off the top of your head. Unlike other crossword puzzles, it's totally okay to cheat. Go ahead and google the titles to discover the name of the author. If you dig more deeply, you just might come up with a little more knowledge of good literature, which might just give your reading list a boost, too!

ACROSS
1. *The Dead Zone*
3. *Cosmos*
5. *War and Peace* (first name)
7. *The Body in the Library*
9. *Masnavi* (poem)
12. *The Lost World*
15. *The Metamorphosis* (last name)
16. *The Color Purple*
19. *Every Last One* (first name)
21. *The Da Vinci Code*
23. *An Essay on Criticism* (last name)
24. *All's Well That Ends Well*
25. *Your Book* (well, if you wrote one)
27. *The Picture of Dorian Gray*
31. *The Republic*
33. *Frankenstein*
34. *The Bourne Identity*
35. *The Things I Love*
38. *A Walk to Remember*
40. *Charlie and the Chocolate Factory* (last name)
41. *The Three Musketeers* (last name)
42. *The Old Man and the Sea* (first name)
43. *Reaching Down the Rabbit Hole* (last name)

DOWN
2. *The Body Farm*
3. *The First Time*
4. *Good Omens*
6. *The Raven*
8. *Think and Grow Rich* (last name)
10. *Frankenstein*
11. *The Complete Saki*
12. *The Handmaid's Tale*
13. This one's not a book title, but you might drink it.
14. *The Bluest Eye*
17. *The Writer in Disguise* (first name)
18. *Safe Harbour*
20. *The Giving Tree*
22. *The Hitchhiker's Guide to the Galaxy* (last name)
26. *To Kill a Mockingbird*
28. *The Old English Baron*
29. *Chiefs* (last name)
30. *Because of Winn-Dixie* (first name)
31. *The Alchemist* (first name)
32. *Odyssey*
34. *The BFG* (first name)
36. *The Mezzanine* (last name)
37. *Aesop's Fables*
39. *The Prince of Tides* (first name)

Writing a Book?

Why? There's really only one good answer to this question: "Because I *want* to." You may have a number of other reasons, like:

- *I love to write.*
- *I am a great writer.*
- *I feel inspired to write.*
- *I want to leave a legacy.*
- *I have a vivid imagination.*
- *I have a message to convey.*
- *I want to teach what I know.*
- *I just came up with a great story idea.*
- *I love exploring my inner world through writing.*
- *I have something to share that I'm passionate about.*
- *Numerous people have told me that I should write a book.*

None of that really matters—especially if you've encountered Writer's Block. The simple fact is if you don't *really* want to do it, chances are you just won't. Writing a good book is a long-term commitment you make to yourself, and you will only commit to what you truly want to do.

List and briefly explain all your reasons for wanting to write a book:

What's your number-one reason?

Are You Being Authentic?

Are you writing on a topic that you know nothing or very little about or from a perspective so different from your own that you're only guessing how such a person would feel? Could that be what's standing in your way today? There's nothing wrong with wanting to step out of your literary comfort zone and/or writing from different perspectives—even if you're stepping into completely uncharted territory—but research is key.

Some genres, like historical fiction and much of nonfiction, require in-depth study to be plausible, both to the reader down the line and to you, the writer. It's important to have a solid understanding of your topic. You're probably not trying to write a how-to book on something you don't know how to do or share any information you don't have a background on. But with fiction it's a little trickier than that. Here's an exercise to help you get to grips with your topic:

What is your genre, and what are the "rules" of that genre?

_____

_____

_____

Are there any tropes of the genre you want to avoid?

_____

_____

_____

What's your setting and time period? What major events are taking place in this time period that would have impacted your characters, directly or indirectly?

What major rules, unspoken or otherwise, might impact how your characters would behave? (For example, are their racial, classist, or gender issues that would affect how your characters interact with each other and the world around them?)

Of the rules above, what rule(s) will your characters need to break to further the plot?

How will your characters move around, and how will your setting impact the speed at which they do so?

> "Cheat your landlord if you can and must, but do not try to shortchange the Muse. It cannot be done. You can't fake quality any more than you can fake a good meal." ~William S. Burroughs

Post a WANTED Sign

What do you need to get past your Writer's Block?

- Your muse?
- Some "free" time?
- Motivation?
- Raw material?
- Trust in the process?
- Confidence as a writer?
- An interested publisher?
- A good editor?
- Something else?

Whatever it is, put it out into the universe by writing or drawing what you need in the circle. Be sure to include a reward too in the space below it—maybe satisfaction, an advance on royalties, pride . . .

Writing Successes & Regrets

Chances are you've written something that has received positive recognition from at least one reader. How about that English essay you wrote in eighth grade? That counts! Now, think about some of your regrets. The novel you started writing when you were 15 and never picked up again after page 10, or that paper you poured your heart and soul into in college and your professor seemed to have an obsession with a red-ink pen? Explore these now:

Write down some of your writing successes and accomplishments:

_____
_____

Now write down some of your regrets—things you started but didn't get to finish.

_____
_____

Focus on your accomplishments and let the regrets go. If there's a lesson you can glean from your regrets, use it to move forward but stop looking back. If you can identify the reason for your successes, do more of that!

> "A professional writer is an amateur who didn't quit." ~Richard Bach

Write Short

If you've got it in your mind that you want to write a book but don't yet have the discipline, commitment, or structure in place, you might find yourself coming up short.

Try setting yourself a shorter writing goal—a short story or an article perhaps. Writing shorter pieces can get you in the writing habit. Plus, it can feel way less daunting than putting pressure on yourself to produce a full-length work on day one. For practice, write one paragraph here, with a clear beginning, middle, and end. Here's an example:

> The truck in the cul-de-sac emitted a back-up warning beep. The dog's ears pricked forward and a sharp bark erupted from his throat—a warning not to disturb the peaceful household on the other side of the hedges. Moments later, the truck drove away. The dog's work was done.

Connectivity Issues

If you aren't connecting to your current writing project, put that project in time-out for a bit and write something else. The key is to keep exercising your writing muscle when what's stopping you is simply not feeling the love for what you're working on.

So what *would* you love to work on? There's no rule that says you've got to write monogamously. Some of the most brilliant minds in history juggled multiple projects at once. It's not about powering through despite the fatigue; it's about keeping your creativity flowing, no matter what tributary it flows into.

Use the facing page to try on something new. First, jot down a few ideas of what you'd like to write instead. Try poetry. If you're usually a poet, try prose. Rewrite a favorite fairy tale. Maybe you're writing a high fantasy but you want to try your hand at a short detective fiction? Give it a go! Write whatever comes to mind—plot, characters, setting, dialogue, etc.—about whatever it is you'd like to try writing.

Break out another notebook if you have to, or a new word-processing doc. Play with this until you miss writing your current project. Whatever this exercise leads you to write, keep it, and keep working on it whenever the mood strikes. By the end, you might just have two completed projects under your writer's belt.

What I'd like to write instead: _____
_____
_____

Now get to it: _____

Switch Off

If what you're working on is just not clicking for you and nobody's breathing down your neck (think *boss, professor, publisher, a demanding fanbase*), try starting another project. Pick something you've had on your mind for a while and maybe even tucked away in your genius folder. Outline it, or just start drafting. Give your "project B" some initial page space by jotting down some notes here:

_____
_____
_____
_____
_____
_____
_____
_____

Now you have two projects to choose between when you sit down to write. Work on the one that excites you at the time. Then, switch off as often as you need to keep the words flowing.

Genius Folder for Fodder

Whether it's an actual folder on your actual desktop or a virtual folder on your virtual desktop, start filling it with ideas, helpful information, inspiring clips, and other useful resources that you can look at when you've encountered a bout of Writer's Block.

By the way, Writer's Block is the perfect time to start a genius folder. Here are a few ideas to get you started:

- Have you read a good article on a topic you're considering writing about? Put a link to the article in your virtual folder or print it out for your actual folder—or both.

- Keep a word file in your genius folder or some loose-leaf pages, and like a detective sleuthing for clues, write down ideas as they come. Flag the ones you really like.

- Does a local haunt inspire you? Snap a picture and squirrel it away in your folder.

- Take a wander through Google image search results or stock photo sites and save what stirs your creative spirit.

> "Imagination is everything. It is the preview of life's coming attractions." ~Albert Einstein

What Comes to Mind?

Without looking ahead, write the first thought that comes to your mind here:

_____

_____

_____

Now the second: _____

_____

_____

Now the third: _____

_____

_____

Now reread what you've written and circle *one* word from each thought statement. Maybe you circled "stupid," "waste," and "unhelpful," or something snarky like that. Or maybe you took this exercise a little more seriously.

Whatever the case, write a new sentence using those three words that has an entirely different meaning from your three thoughts. If you've circled any verbs, any form of the verb will do.

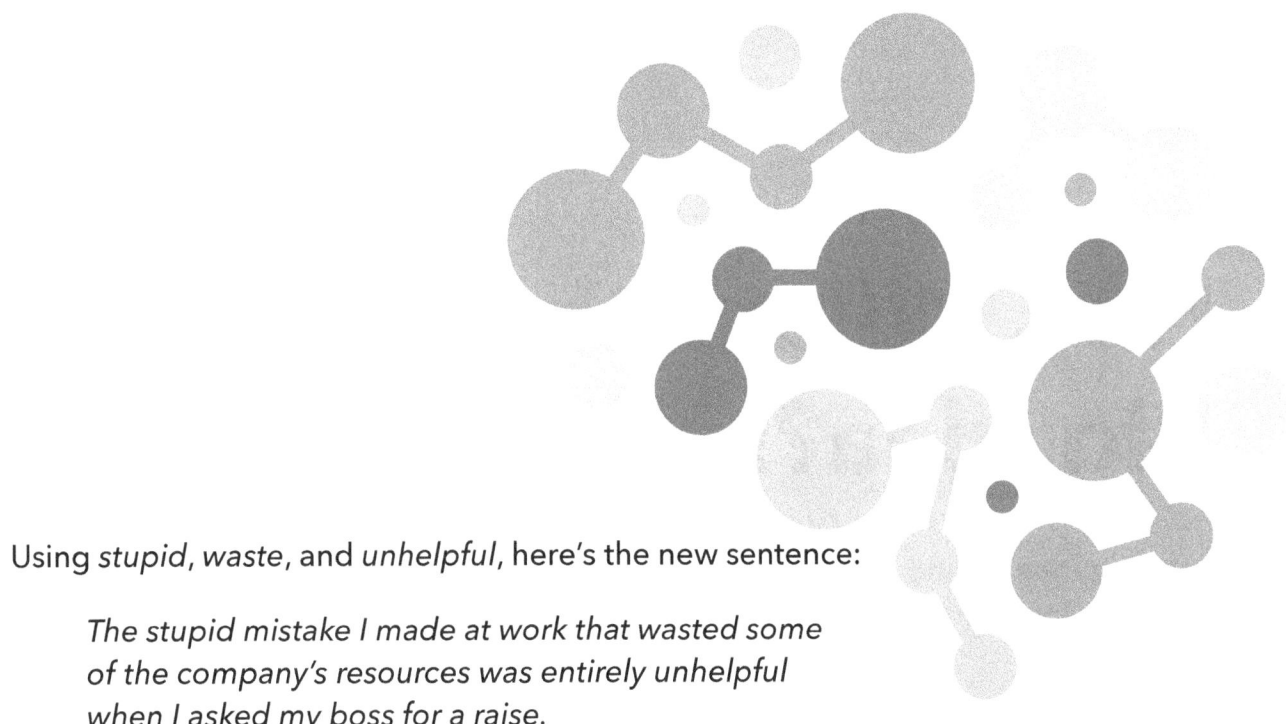

Using *stupid*, *waste*, and *unhelpful*, here's the new sentence:

The stupid mistake I made at work that wasted some of the company's resources was entirely unhelpful when I asked my boss for a raise.

Write your new sentence here:

_____

_____

_____

Notice how the new sentence using the snark words creates an opportunity to fill in even more information. What *was* that stupid mistake? What industry do I work in? Did my boss throw my mistake in my face? And so on and so on.

Just pulling random words out of your head and playing around with them in a sentence can spark your imagination.

Hey, What's the Big Idea?!

Your big idea should be fueling your writing sessions, so if you don't have one, you may be trying to drive your car without a destination—or, worse yet, without fuel in your gas tank.

Of course, if it works for you to sit down and write without a big idea in mind, that's great. Maybe you're simply going for a joy ride and your destination will reveal itself as if by magic. But maybe not.

- If you're writing nonfiction, what do you want to impart to your reader through your chosen topic? How is it different from other writing on that same topic? Why would the reader choose your work to learn about this topic over others? Do you have a secret formula or unique way of presenting the information?

- If you're writing fiction, what's your genre? Who are your characters? What's your setting? What's the incident that incites your characters into action? What are the end goals? What's in the way? What about your story is unique?

With those questions in mind, see if you can describe your prospective work in one paragraph without getting into the nitty-gritty details:

_____
_____
_____
_____
_____
_____
_____
_____
_____
_____

Rework this idea as much as you need to until it revs your engine, and then get on the road to writing. *Happy trails to you!*

Stretch

Do you think you'd do your best writing if you felt loose and relaxed or rigid and uptight? The answer's a no-brainer, right? Obviously, the more relaxed you feel, the more you're likely to produce something worth reading.

Get into a routine of stretching before you sit down to write and then take brief stretching breaks throughout your writing session.

Not sure how to stretch without pulling something? Watch some YouTube videos. You may even want to do some yoga poses before sitting down to write. It's more involved than stretching, but it can also keep your body—and mind—limber.

New to yoga? YouTube is the way. In fact, type "yoga for writers" into the search bar for some great options, tailored especially for your craft.

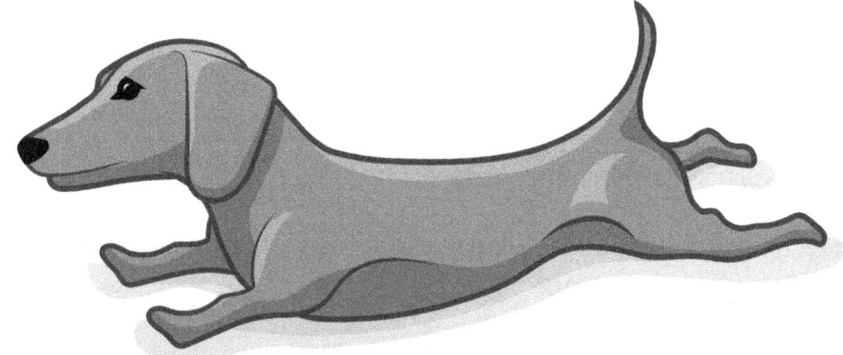

Work Out Something Other Than Your Brain

Have you ever felt a spark of creative inspiration during a workout? Some creative types claim that whole ideas have "downloaded" into their brain while they were focusing on their body's movements during a workout. Whether or not your next best idea suddenly pops into your head, it's been established that exercise can boost your mood—and when you're dealing with the frustration of Writer's Block, even a small improvement can help.

If you are usually sedentary—as many writers are—consult a physician or trainer before going gung ho on a new exercise routine. For now, let's look at a bunch of "beginner" activities. If you don't have any physical limitations or contraindications (but you do have the necessary equipment), spend 10 minutes doing one of these now and then sit back down to write to see if the movement helps.

- Brisk walking
- Bike riding or spinning (think, "spin bike" not "twirling in place")
- Jumping on a trampoline or jumping rope
- Rollerblading
- Jogging or running

Start Vague

You might be blocked by the notion that your ideas need to be fully fleshed out to be worth something. But that's not necessarily true. Sure, the details need to be there . . . eventually, but a vague idea that you can build upon is an excellent starting position.

Think of it this way: If you're making a cake, you don't start with a fully baked one. You must first have the idea to bake a cake, and then gather the ingredients and put them together in just the right order and place it in the oven at just the right temperature for just the right length of time.

What are some of your vague ideas? Note a couple here:

_____

_____

_____

_____

_____

Of these vague ideas, which one do you think has the most potential? Get ready to bake that one. Start by gathering the details until you have some tasty batter.

Having trouble? Put it in the deep freeze for now and try fleshing out another vague idea—or keep coming up with vague ideas that you may want to gather ingredients for later. You may even want to link some of your vague ideas for the start of a delicious triple-layer cake.

Establish Your Priorities

Do you write *only* after you've done *everything* else on your to-do list? Then, when it comes time to sit down and write, all you really want to do is binge on some TV shows and then go to bed? You know what that means? It means you haven't made writing a priority.

Change your mindset. Just because whatever you're writing isn't making money (yet, that is, hopefully!) doesn't mean it's not worth being treated with the same dedication as a job that brings in a paycheck.

Consider what on your to-do list could, realistically, be done *after* you've taken the time to write. Getting to work on time, doing the laundry, and washing the dishes are all priorities, but maybe rearranging your bookshelves can take a backseat for now. If all goes well, you'll need to rearrange those shelves again anyway . . . to make room for your book!

Write the top-10 items on your to-do list. Make sure you include your writing! Now, thinking objectively, consider which non-writing items could come after you've written. Unless you're completely out of underwear, perhaps the laundry can wait another day.

1. _____
2. _____
3. _____
4. _____
5. _____
6. _____
7. _____
8. _____
9. _____
10. _____

"Trust in what you love, continue to do it, and it will take you where you need to go."
~Natalie Goldberg

Write What You ♥

Are you having a love affair with your ideas? If your writing isn't going anywhere, it's probably them, not you.

Perhaps you're focused on writing what other people love, but you're just not that into it. It's time to really look at what makes you feel passionate. Let your mind wander, and spend a few minutes scanning your thoughts. Notice your visceral emotional reactions to the ideas that come up. What flutters your butterflies?

I feel passionate about:

1. _____
2. _____
3. _____
4. _____
5. _____

Once you've identified a few of your passions, play around with exploring one or more of them in a piece of writing. If you must, let your ho-hum ideas down easily as you set off on this new love affair.

Adopt a New Role

If nothing's come out of *your* head, put on someone else's "head" by writing from an entirely new perspective. When you sit down to write, imagine you are:

- A different gender
- 20 years older or younger
- An extraterrestrial with a limited understanding of Earth
- A barnyard animal
- A mosquito
- Incredibly wealthy or completely destitute
- A piece of paper
- A sun, moon, quasar, or another celestial object
- An electron

Pretending you are someone (or something) else can give your mind the wiggle room to produce something refreshing. When you're all done, take your expanded perspective to the page you *must* write next.

Try on one of these perspectives now, set a timer for 10 minutes, and see what you come up with:

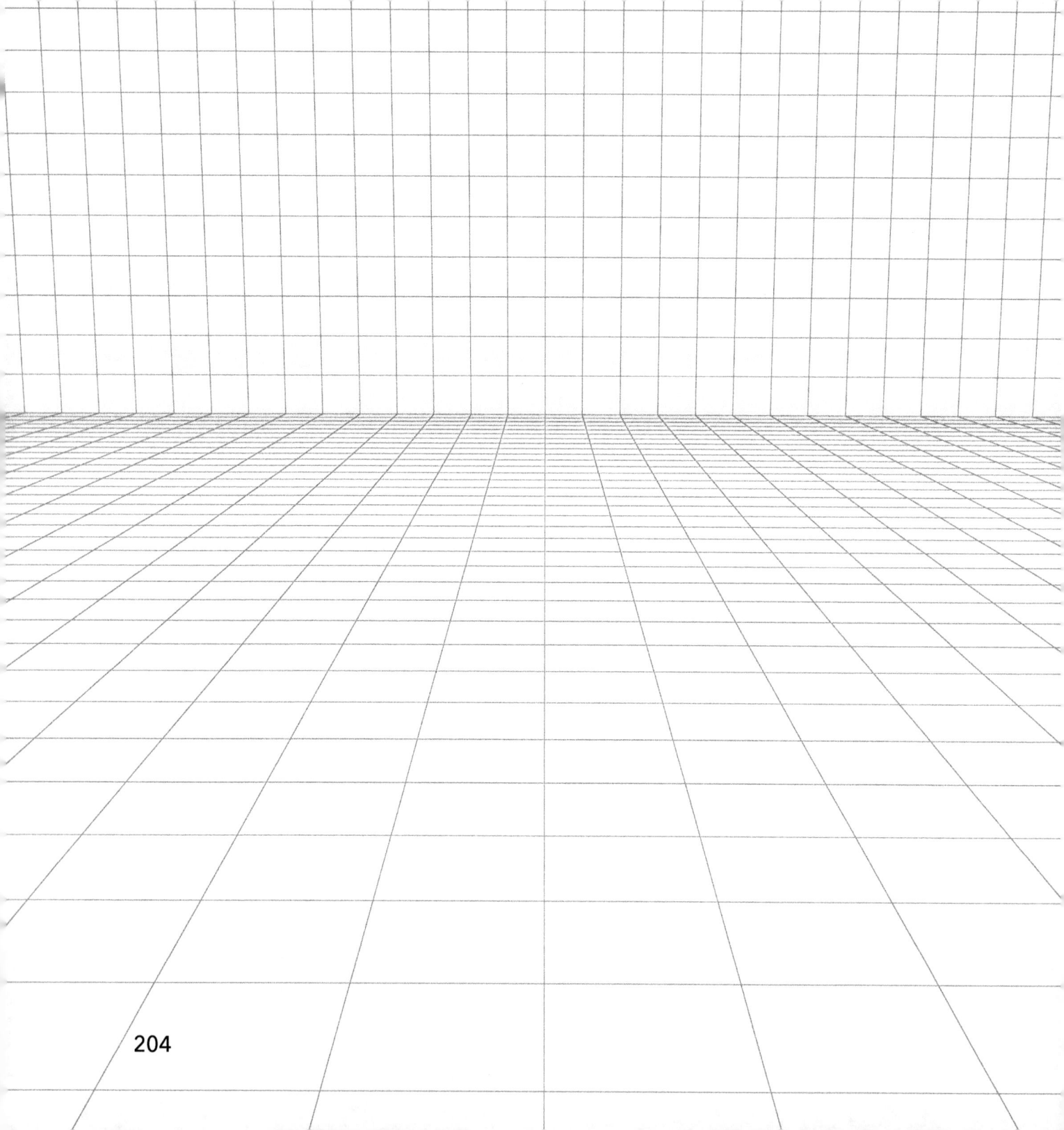

Expand Your Perspective

Do you have a narrow view of your writer's life and what you "can" and "can't" do when it comes to writing? For instance, do you think you can only write . . .

- Nonfiction or fiction but not both?
- In one particular genre?
- About realistic situations?
- Short stories but not a whole book?
- For children but not for adults or vice versa?
- Prose but not poetry or vice versa?
- Standalone books but never a series?

If you relate to any of these, take your blinders off and give something you *think* you can't write a whirl. Your Writer's Block may be a sign that it's time to try something new.

Take a crack at whatever genre is the farthest out of your comfort zone. Why not that nonfiction topic you know a lot about but never tried writing? Learn how to write a haiku. Outline a series! Broadening your perspective might just unlock some creative potential you never knew you had.

Put on Your Thinking Cap

Ever thought of putting on your thinking cap (beyond kindergarten)? Just like a vision board can stimulate you visually and the right music provides auditory inspiration, putting on an inspiring piece of clothing can help you achieve a writerly mindset.

It's not much of a stretch, really. Maybe your granddad's flat cap makes you feel secure, which can make the words flow more easily if you wear it when you write. Maybe it's a tiara that gives you a royal flair or a simple baseball cap or cozy winter hat with the pompom. Or maybe your thinking cap isn't a cap at all. Maybe it's your favorite hoodie or T-shirt or cozy pair of socks.

Don't have a thinking cap sitting around? You can make a thinking cap using a plain hat and whatever paint, glitter, buttons, stickers, feathers, or pins strike your fancy. Don't want to go through all the trouble? Well, there's always the old tried-and-true imaginary hat that you used in kindergarten.

Now, before you sit down to write, put on your thinking cap and feel the words flowing from your brain into your fingers.

"A little nonsense now and then is relished by the wisest men." ~Willy Wonka in *Willy Wonka and the Chocolate Factory*

Helpline

Call a good friend (one who is normally caring and supportive). Don't call a *writer* friend—you don't want them to catch your Writer's Block. 😊

Ask if they have 15 minutes to listen to you, and if so, tell them the idea you're stuck on. Talk out what you want to write. Keep a notepad in front of you to doodle or write down key phrases about what you're sharing.

The simple act of talking about it can help you find focus and clarity, and who knows, your non-writer friend might have some useful feedback to help you get past this temporary obstacle. Take notes on what they say, too. Those notes might prove helpful.

If you prefer to text, all this brainstorming will be at your fingertips, but talking it out will likely give you a different perspective.

Drowning in Digital Distractions

You sit down to write. Your laptop is open with a fresh page waiting for your words, and your phone is beside you. You put your fingers on the keyboard, and a text message comes in. It pops up on your phone and maybe even on your laptop message app, too.

It's a link to a cute video of goats in pajamas, so you watch. How could you not? Why do goats even wear pajamas? Your browser is waiting in the background, so you google it. You don't actually find a straightforward answer, but there are ton of other baby goat videos, with *and* without pajamas. Now, what were you just about to write when that text message chimed?

Facebook. What's everyone up to?

Your e-mail chimes, Facebook is open, and you check your mail. It's a $4,396 bill for a service you are certain you didn't use, so you go back to your browser to search if it's a scam.

There's a notification on your Facebook. Someone liked or commented on one of your posts. You click to see their reaction. Wait. Are you really that self-centered? No. So you look at the newsfeed and react to a couple of things. Another e-mail comes in. Another text message chimes. Someone just commented on your comment.

Thirty-two minutes later, and you still haven't confirmed that the $4,396 bill was a scam nor have you written a word. Must be Writer's Block. Ahhhh! It happens to the best of us, but it's totally avoidable.

When you sit down to write (actually, *before* you sit down to write), try this:

1. Put your phone on "Do Not Disturb." If you're worried about missing something important, you can set up your phone to send all calls to voicemail except for a certain numbers (think *kids, significant other, parents,* and *best friend*).

2. Place your phone across the room.

3. Shut down your e-mail program. (Check e-mails only after your writing session is complete.)

4. Open your word-processing program, and close all other nonessential applications and programs.

5. Avoid your browser at all costs. Need to check the online dictionary or the thesaurus? Wait until the last half hour of your writing session so you don't "accidentally" click on a social media platform instead. Use brackets to hold the space (see page 20).

Seriously. It's that easy to avoid the digital distractions that keep you from writing. If you don't feel comfortable without checking social media every so often, even during your writing sessions, maybe it's time for a digital detox.

Short on "Newsfeed" Content?

It's OK if a book, article, essay, or even a blog isn't in your future—Writer's Block doesn't discriminate. So maybe you just want to create compelling social-media posts to engage with your audience. This is where you need to get to the heart of the matter: your heart.

Do you believe 100% in your product and/or services?

If you want to start with a strong foundation, believing in what you have to offer is essential. With that foundation in place, ask yourself:

Why am I so passionate about this?

_____

_____

How is what I'm offering different from what's already available?

_____

_____

What's the benefit to my audience?

_____

_____

And, for that matter, who is my audience?

_____

_____

Clear answers to those key questions can uproot the block that's holding you back from establishing a captivating social-media presence through:

- Developing your brand
- Sharing your story
- Creating engaging video clips, live and recorded
- Asking thought-provoking questions
- Posting compelling images and infographics
- Reposting interesting articles
- Making big announcements
- Hosting an exciting contest
- Simply sharing your authentic voice

Whether it's book length or limited to 280 characters, creating content for your social-media platform takes time, commitment, consistency, and above all, belief in yourself and what you have to offer.

Embrace the WIP

What does every published work have in common with what you're writing now? It was once a work in progress (WIP). You don't just sit down at your computer and write a finished piece from the get-go. Michelangelo took three years to sculpt the statue of David. Imagine if he didn't embrace the work-in-progress part of the process? We'd be *oohing* and *ahhing* over a chunk of marble with so much unrealized potential.

Think of writing like sculpting out a breathtaking story or riveting work of nonfiction. You start with a vision and "chip away" in big chunks at first to make room for later refinement. When you start chipping away at your Writer's Block with diligence, something noteworthy will emerge.

Leaving on a Thought Plane

Doubting your ability? Questioning your every phrase? For every word you type, do you feel like you're hitting the "Delete" key three times over? It's time to send your inner critic off on a vacation. Go someplace where you won't be disturbed, close your eyes, and try this:

1. Think of the most relaxing destination you can imagine—the farther away the better. A tropical island will do.

2. Buy a ticket with a virtual airline and book a virtual room overlooking the ocean at an upscale resort with unlimited beverages and buffets.

3. Call a virtual cab and walk your inner critic to the door, baggage and all.

4. Wave goodbye. Visualize your inner critic arriving at their destination and having the time of their life. Don't expect them back until it's time to make revisions.

A harsh inner critic can stop you in your tracks, for sure, but being critical of your own work can also help you improve it. As long as you don't take this to the extreme (and your inner critic isn't a *total* jerk), you can listen to its feedback the way you would to other people's and then put it in perspective. In other words, take anything that's helpful and leave the rest behind.

How To . . .

If you had to name one thing you are really great at, what would it be? Think beyond writing. Maybe you make a mean chili or you're great at juggling. Perhaps you have a flair for fashion or photography. Got that in mind? It's time to share your expertise with your fans.

Think about everything that's involved in the process of what you do well, and then explain to a neophyte how to go about doing it. If this is your first foray into "how-to," imagine that you are explaining the process to a child.

You're going to need some room to really explore this, so open a new word-processing document, and begin, well, at the beginning. Tell the reader why this topic is close to your heart, what you hope they'll gain from your knowledge, what supplies they need to get started, and then move on to step 1. Fully explain the process step by step until you believe the reader could potentially do what you are teaching them to do.

> "The true alchemists do not change lead into gold; they change the world into words." ~William H. Gass

Time Travel

Take a trip forward in time to your ideal future as a writer. Then, write a letter to your future self, telling Older You how impressed you are that you snapped out of your Writer's Block and produced the MASTERPIECE you'd always dreamed of starting . . . and finishing. Shower Future You with well-deserved praise.

Dear Future Me,

_____

_____

_____

_____

_____

_____

_____

_____

Love,

My Present Self

Power Lines

"It was a dark and stormy night."

You might think Snoopy from the *Peanuts* was the first to use that now-cliché phrase, but it was actually English writer Edward Bulwer-Lytton in the novel *Paul Clifford,* which was published in 1830. Sure, it's become the butt of jokes, but it was memorable enough to make it into our collective consciousness. Here's another you are surely familiar with: "Once upon a time."

While you don't want to fall back on either of those two phrases to start your book, you do want your first line to hook not only your reader's attention but also yours: first and foremost, *yours*. Why? Because it will make you want to continue writing, and it will make them want to continue reading.

A good first line may be the jolt of energy you need to get your creative juices flowing. What are the qualities that go into a good first line? Here are a few:

- ✔ Vivid
- ✔ Bold
- ✔ Striking
- ✔ Engaging
- ✔ Distinct
- ✔ Clear

While you might decide to change your first line after revisions, get off on the right foot by coming up with an opener that reflects the incredible power of the written word. You want to avoid touching powerlines out in the wild, but touch as many as you can come up with here:

Day Job Distractions

Lots of writers have "day jobs," and as we all know, many of these day jobs leak into evenings and weekends. Maybe your coworkers text you to gripe, or maybe your boss emails you with tasks they expect you to tackle on Monday. Unless you've already agreed to extra at-home work, these distractions can leave you scrambling to accomplish all your off-day tasks, which means your writing may take a backseat if you're not protective of your creative time.

Here are some tips to combat that day-job overspill.

- ✔ Have one folder designated "For Work" on your personal desktop. Any and all work files go in that folder. Make sure you update it as needed, but don't crowd your personal desktop with work stuff.

- ✔ Don't store your creative writing on your work computer. Your desk at work is not the place to store material that could distract you, just like your personal computer shouldn't be cluttered with work-related files that can distract you from writing.

- ✔ When you're on the clock, avoid writing anything longer than a quick note-to-self. You could write on a lunchbreak, but set an alarm so you don't surpass your allowed break time. Taking your "work work" as seriously as your "writing work" will help you establish the right mindset to accomplish each with the same level of dedication.

- ✔ At a certain point in the evening on a workday, stop checking work emails and texts. This will not only provide you the structure to stick to a writing schedule, but it will also establish boundaries with your colleagues. If they want their emails and texts answered, they'll learn not to send them at 11 PM on a Saturday.

- ✔ When you have a day off and need to deal with your work email, designate a time of day to check in. If you have more than one day off in a row, perhaps check your mail at the end of the day, as by then all the related emails will have come in. Respond to all that you can respond to in one sitting, and then leave them alone until you either return to the office or until your designated email check-in time the next day.

- ✔ As much as possible, treat your writing with the same level of commitment and dedication as you would a second job. You wouldn't answer emails from your "other" boss on company time at your second job, so while you're writing, leave those texts and emails alone. If anyone asks you why you didn't respond, tell them the truth: You were working. Writing is work. Just because you're presently hammering out a work in progress doesn't make it any less valuable.

Just about every writer nowadays has responsibilities outside of writing. It's OK to let those responsibilities take precedence when the situation calls for it—just as long as writing reports doesn't replace the "real" writing you want to do.

What a Character!

If your characters aren't engaging you enough to keep writing about them, it may be that you just don't know them well enough. A great way to get to know your characters better is to map out *everything* about them—even their subconscious motivations and external influences.

Here's a shortcut to help you make your characters more three-dimensional:

1. Choose a birthdate for your character, a time of birth, and a place of birth. If they were born off world, that's OK. Just choose any time and place on earth that feels like a good fit.

2. Google "free natal chart" or "free birth chart" and choose among the offerings.

3. Enter the details requested, and voila, you have a detailed map of your character's personality, including their strengths, weaknesses, propensities, drives, fears, lessons to learn, relationships with others, and more. This isn't written in stone (just the stars), so you can take from it just what you feel gives your character more life.

Try a few different websites to find a freebie that works best for you. If you like this idea, you can also download a paid app for more astrological details like your character's daily horoscope. Stuck on the direction of the scene? What do the stars say your character is up against today?

Create a new character now. Maybe you'll work them into a story someday or maybe they will live and die on this page.

Character's name: _____

Birthdate: _____

Time of birth: _____

Place of birth: _____

Sun sign: _____

Strengths: _____

_____

Weaknesses:_____

_____

Other relevant info:

_____

_____

_____

_____

"You can make anything by writing." ~C. S. Lewis

Plant Your Garden

You're probably expecting this to be about your metaphorical garden—you know, planting the seeds of inspiration and then watching them bloom into flowers of ideas. Nope. That's not what this is. This is about planting an *actual* garden—even if it's just on your windowsill.

Caring for your green space can serve as a much-needed getaway from your writer's nook. A half hour of gardening or even just taking a few moments to water and talk to your indoor plant can help your mind relax enough to soften the edges of your Writer's Block.

What's more, mindfully nurturing something other than your frustration can help you feel purposeful and accomplished, and when you're feeling those feelings, you can carry them back to your desk. Hold on to them as you set your fingers back on your keyboard.

If you don't have a green thumb, you can tend to the garden on the facing page instead by coloring it in a little at a time.

30-Day Lifetime Challenge

If you officially challenge yourself to write every day, you might be able to write yourself right out of your Writer's Block. (Yes, sometimes that works.) Get yourself a notebook for this activity and label the cover "30-Day Lifetime Challenge" in bold marker to make it official.

Each day, set aside at least a half hour to respond to the prompt, writing from any viewpoint you choose. There's no pressure here. You're only working on a rough draft. If you want to refine what you write later, great, but the challenge here is to simply create a first draft for each of the following:

- **DAY 1:** You're a spark of energy, full of potential.
- **DAY 2:** You're a baby in the womb, comfortable but curious.
- **DAY 3:** You're in the process of being born and discover the outside world.
- **DAY 4:** You are given a new stuffed toy, the one that will become your favorite.
- **DAY 5:** You are on the playground with bigger kids, noticing how little you are.
- **DAY 6:** You start school, meet your teacher and classmates, and make a friend who will become your lifelong bestie.
- **DAY 7:** It's the first day of summer vacation.
- **DAY 8:** You celebrate your tenth birthday.
- **DAY 9:** You get a big part in the school play.

DAY 10: You and your family move to a new home.

DAY 11: You discover the cliques in middle school.

DAY 12: You get in big trouble for doing something you shouldn't have done.

DAY 13: You have a crush on a classmate who doesn't seem to know you exist.

DAY 14: You go to your first dance.

DAY 15: You have a fight with your best friend.

DAY 16: You have your first kiss.

DAY 17: You start high school, feeling like a small fish in a big pond.

DAY 18: You get your first part-time job.

DAY 19: You're packing to go off to college.

DAY 20: You celebrate your twentieth-first birthday.

DAY 21: You go backpacking with your friends.

DAY 22: You meet your future spouse.

DAY 23: You start your career.

DAY 24: You have a baby.

DAY 25: You celebrate your first child's wedding.

DAY 26: You hold your grandbaby for the first time.

DAY 27: You are celebrating your retirement.

DAY 28: You travel to interesting places.

DAY 29: You're dying, surrounded by loved ones and that toy from day 4.

DAY 30: You're dead.

Fuel Up!

Do you get hangry if you haven't eaten recently? Your coffee cup might be full, but your brain can't operate on caffeine alone. Just like a plane needs jet fuel to transport its passengers to exciting places, your brain needs nutrients to transport your thoughts to the page and eventually to your readers' eyes.

When your brain is short on fuel, chances are it's going to cancel all your upcoming flights. Maybe you're grounded right now, and that's why you're reading this. If so, it's time to figure out what your body needs to get back up in the air.

You probably know about the basics of nutrition, which is a good thing because this isn't a book about what or how to eat. Don't know the best brain-boosting foods? Look them up, and then make it your next task to plan out your meals to be sure that when you sit down to write, your brain and body are operating on high-quality "jet fuel." Then, keep a healthy snack within reach while you write in case you need some lift during your flight.

Can You See the Finish Line?

Imagine participating in a race with no end point. You just keep running and running, maybe even in circles. If this feels like what you're doing when it comes to writing, you'll want to establish a "finish line"—a specific, time-bound end point that's realistic, doable, and trackable.

Write your specific goal here: _____

_____

_____

Here's an example: Write a 45,000-word, 10-chapter manuscript with an introduction and conclusion on X topic or about X.

Is it a realistic (that is, do you have the know-how)? _____

If you put in the time, is it doable? _____

How will you track your progress from start to finish? _____

_____

_____

When do you realistically think you can complete this project? _____

Move the Finish Line (if you can)

You're in the middle of the writing race, nearing the finish line, and then suddenly, *Wham!* You trip over a rock in your path (maybe it's a Writer's Block).

Remember the finish line you established on the previous page? It's time to move it. Considering you've lost some ground, when do you realistically think you can complete this project now?_____

If you've established your own finish line, moving it is a perfectly acceptable option. We all stumble from time to time. But, if you're answering to someone else, that finish line may actually be set in stone. What do you need to do now?

- Ask for more time?
- Double down on the time you have remaining?
- Find someone who can help you?
- Something else? Brainstorm here:

_____
_____
_____

Half-Baked Ideas

You're sitting at your keyboard, thinking about . . . well, nothing. You have an idea of what you want to write, but it's not fully baked yet. Should you just sit there and hope the words come? If that hasn't helped in the past, it's probably not going to help now. Now's a good time to engage in an alternate activity that may actually help metaphorically. Yes, bake something. A cake, bread, cookies, cupcakes . . .

1. Find a recipe you like and gather the ingredients.

2. As you follow the instructions, imagine that each ingredient you add represents an aspect of your writing project.

3. As you mix the ingredients, imagine your words coming together on the page, blending into one cohesive ball of a document.

4. Spoon the batter onto or into the baking dish, and set the kitchen timer. While your treat is baking, close your eyes and think about your idea, turning it over in your mind until the timer goes off.

5. Take it out of the oven to cool. Set the timer again for the recommended cooling time, and revisit your idea until your treat is ready to eat.

6. Grab a slice, cookie, or cupcake, and head back to your writing desk. Take a yummy bite, and write what you thought about.

A Word Break

Ever tried your hand at sudoku? Give your mind a short break from trying to produce words by working with numbers and logic instead. In this puzzle, each row, column, and outlined square (all made up of 9 spaces each) must contain the numbers 1 through 9 without repeating any number in that row, column, or square.

1				2				8
			3		4			
		2				5		
	4			3			2	
	7						5	
	8	3	6	4	2	7	9	
	2						8	
	3			7			1	
8	1	9				2	7	5

(The solution's on page 298.)

Shower for Power

Sometimes it makes total creative sense to roll right out of bed in the morning and jump on the computer to start jotting down the fresh inspiration of a new day. The expectation that your words will flow first thing may have even become a habit you rely on. It may also be a habit that's seen better days.

> Feeling fresh can power you up for the writing day ahead. Before you get down to the business of writing, take a steamy shower. Incorporate your favorite pick-me-up aroma, like of peppermint or eucalyptus, into the steam by using a shower steamer or just putting a few drops of the essential oil on a washcloth and leave it under the flow of the water.
>
> While you're in the shower, let your mind wander as it will. Take care of business, and let the business of creativity take care of itself.

▶ There's no need to wait till morning to shower—and it's perfectly okay to shower more than once in a day! So, if you're having a particularly bad case of Writer's Block, see if a midday or evening shower is the rejuvenating break you need to get your words flowing again.

Connect the Dots for Clarity

If you're lacking clarity around a topic or idea, start by connecting the dots. Try this:

1. Spend a few minutes thinking about what you want to write. What are some key terms or ideas that come to mind?

2. Give each key term or idea its own bullet point (aim for 10). For each of these, write a simple sentence that encapsulates the message or information you want to share.

3. Arrange your bullets in a logical sequence. For example, do you need to understand a concept before you can understand another? Does one event need to take occur before something else can happen?

4. Take this a step further by creating sub-bullets. For example, maybe your first key term is "Writer's Block" and your sentence reads "There are many possible causes of writer's block." You might have sub-bullets that read *fatigue, lack of inspiration, fear* . . .

5. Create full sentences for each of your sub-bullets. If additional topics fall under that sub-bulleted item, take it down another level by creating additional bullet points and pairing those with complete sentences.

6. Keep connecting the dots by drawing a line (in the form of words, of course!) from idea to idea until you reveal the complete picture.

Connect These Dots

Draw a line connecting all the dots to every other dot.
This is way more involved than it looks.

(The solution's on page 298.)

A Room with a New View

You've got your cozy writer's den just the way you want it. Your vision board is hanging on the wall in front of you, fresh water and snacks await your fingertips in case you need some sustenance, and the temperature is just right—in fact, the setting couldn't be better. But you can't write a dang word today.

Get up. Get out. And take your laptop or notepad with you. Just because you can't write at your desk doesn't mean you can't write at your kitchen table, out on the patio, or even in your parked car.

How Do I Love Thee?

What do you absolutely love about writing? Do you love the click of the keys or the scratch of the pen? Do you love seeing the thoughts in your head become words on paper? Do you love expressing your innermost desires and imaginings? Do you love the clarity of the written word? Remembering why you love writing can be a powerful impetus for getting back to it. Write your love letter here:

Dear Writing:

I love you because _____

_____

_____

_____

_____

_____

_____

_____

Love,

_____
your name

Grounding

Writers spend a lot of time in their heads where it's easy to get lost. If you're wandering around aimlessly in your headspace, it's a good idea to ground yourself—that is, bring your awareness back to your body in its place on earth where you can take a deep breath, reorient yourself, and get back on track. Here's a simple way to get grounded:

1. Weather permitting, go outside and take off your shoes and socks. Stand up straight with your arms hanging at your sides.

2. Feel your feet standing firmly on the earth. Notice how every part of your foot touches the ground, keeping you stable. Press in with your right foot and then with your left, finding balance between the two.

3. Close your eyes if you'd like to. Feel the sun on your skin and the air around you. Hear the sounds of nature, honking cars included.

4. Take a deep breath as if you are pulling energy from the earth up through your body and into your lungs. Hold it for a moment, and then release. Take a few breaths like this, noting what you smell as you breathe in.

5. Open your eyes. Shake your arms, roll your shoulders and then your hips, and shake each leg out.

6. Spend another moment being fully present to all your body sensations. You are grounded in this moment.

▶ If you can't go outside, try this exercise indoors. There are other grounding exercises, too. Do an online search for one that you like and practice whenever you get lost in the woods of your mind.

Emotional Overload

If you're having a particularly emotional day and can't find your focus, take a few minutes to yourself before you sit down to write. Talking about your feelings with another person might be next up on your agenda, but if it's simply a case of wanting to find some peace so you can write with renewed focus, try this:

What are you feeling? Name as many emotions as you recognize yourself having:

_____

_____

1. Find a comfy chair, close your eyes if you'd like, and take a few deep breaths.
2. Notice where in your body you are feeling the emotion(s). For example, you might feel it in your head, heart, and/or stomach.
3. Place your attention on the physical feeling, and breathe a few times as you focus on that area. After a few minutes, speak to the emotion. For example, "Hey, anticipation, I notice you, and it makes sense that you are here. I feel you. You can come back later, but right now, I'd like to focus on my writing."
4. Now, imagine that your emotion responds. It might say, "OK, see you later" or maybe it says, "I'm done here." Have it say something to you that lets you off the hook, at least for now.
5. Take a few more deep breaths, and say thanks. If you are feeling more than one emotion (as is often the case), repeat the process.

▶ If you still don't feel like writing because of what you're feeling, maybe it is time to talk to someone or just take a little more quiet time with yourself to fully process what you're feeling.

Say What You Gotta Write

Have you ever shared your idea with someone who listens in wonder as the words flow effortlessly from your mouth, and then as soon as you sit down to write about it, you can't remember a word of what you said? It happens. You wish you had all that recorded so you can go back and listen. Thanks to technology, you can do just that and then some.

If you have the Google Docs app and your phone has a voice-to-text function, you can dictate directly into Google Docs, which you can open either on your phone or on your computer's internet browser to edit. This is great if you tend to forget to back up your files.

You can also purchase an MP3 recorder if voice-to-text doesn't resonate with you, or you can download dictation software to your computer to type as you talk. You could also pay a transcription service to convert your spoken words to written words. Your word-processing program might even have a dictate function.

Whatever option you choose, consider this voice-to-text material only as rough copy to work with. Also, read the transcription carefully because sometimes similar-sounding words (e.g., "Sirius") may be substituted for the word you said ("serious"), Siriusly.

Let Go of the Guilt

There are some writers who feel guilty for *not* writing, but that's not the kind of guilt we're talking about here. This is about feeling guilty *for* writing, as you might think:

- You *should* be doing other stuff.
- You *should not* be "wasting" your time writing.
- You *should* be outside enjoying the day.

You may have your own version of these thoughts, but they all boil down to one thing: You feel guilty for nurturing this part of your life. Admit it. That's a good first step to letting it go. Feel it. That's a good second step. And then put it in perspective.

For you, writing is a creative outlet, and it's something you are drawn to do. As long as your house isn't crumbling around you, you have food on the table when necessary, you hold down a job if you have one, and you care for those who aren't capable of caring for themselves (think, kids and animal companions), there's absolutely no reason not to spend your scheduled "free" time writing.

I, _____, give myself permission to write. I write because:

_____

_____

_____

These are all valid reasons.

Sincerely, _____

People Watch

Need some inspiration for the characters in your story? Head over to your local coffee shop, order something, and sit in an inconspicuous corner. Then:

- Observe the interactions between the baristas and the customers.

- Notice the different styles of dress and the shapes, sizes, and features of the individuals.

- Notice their body language and mannerisms and think about what those behaviors might suggest.

- If a particular person catches your attention, give them a backstory: What brought them here to this very moment? Think ahead, too: What are they going to do this evening?

Take notes on everything you observe and any scenarios you imagine. You don't need to limit this to the coffee shop, of course. Put on your writer's cap whenever you go out and notice people with the intention of becoming an expert on human nature so that you can write three-dimensional characters.

Field Notes:

If you need more room, use the blanks in the back.

Learn to Juggle

Think of yourself as a juggler. You can only have two balls in your hands at once, while all the others are up in the air. How many balls are you currently juggling? Think health, family, work, home life, social life, hobbies and recreation, community, spirituality/religion, and finances. Let's add another: writing.

Each of your balls needs some "palm time." Much of the other balls we're juggling require the bulk of our time. We can't just drop things like our work schedule, our family's needs, or our financial obligations. But how often is your writing getting the palm time it needs?

Professional jugglers know that rhythm is an important part of successful juggling. If you find you can't seem to catch that writing ball, maybe your rhythm—that is, your time management—is the issue. Fill in the circles on the facing page with the names of the balls you're juggling. You can draw more as needed. Write the approximate time you spend each week "palming" each of these in the circle, too. Now, number the balls in order of importance—and make sure writing time is in there!

Which ones could you give a little less palm time to? For example, if you host a weekly game night, maybe you could ask someone else to host one week a month so you can take a night off to write. Color the balls that could take a little less time in green.

Which ones are you inconsistently palming? Maybe you plan your meals the day of. What if you spent an hour a week to create a menu to save yourself the mental labor every day? How much time would you save digging in the cabinets trying to throw dinner together? Color those balls you could give more consistent attention to in red.

Of the balls remaining, which ones aren't getting enough attention? Color those in blue. If your finances are piling up and you find yourself having to drop other balls to scramble to pick up your finances, it's time to adjust your schedule to make time to palm that ball.

Ideas Bubbling Up

Stir the pot of your ideas with this bubble-up brainstorming exercise. Set aside 20 minutes for this activity to give yourself plenty of time to brainstorm. Here's how:

In the center bubble, jot down your main topic. For instance, "how to get over writer's block." Think of ideas for subtopics, and write them in the outlying bubbles. For instance, *self-care, structure, alternative mental activities, writing prompts, physical activity/exercise, perspective-switching, reducing distractions,* and *support*. This is an excellent start to an outline for writing a book on overcoming writer's block, don't you think?

But what if you're not writing a how-to or some other nonfiction work? Fiction can be more complex, depending on your genre, and you needn't encompass a whole work in a bubble map. Try stirring around different aspects of your story to work out ideas.

- Make character bubbles. Write a character's name in the center and fill the surrounding bubbles with personality traits, physical attributes, languages spoken, family background, favorite foods, and so on. Even if some of these traits never make it to the page, they may shape how you write that character's thoughts, dialogue, and actions.

- Struggling to put your plot points in coherent order? Bubble map your plot! Write your start point in one bubble and your end point in the center. Write key plot points in the remaining bubbles, adding more as needed. Once you've jotted in all your key plot points, draw arrows to connect them. (This is an alternative to the figure shown.)

- Writing a new universe? Write its name in the middle and key aspects of it in the outer bubbles. You can even add smaller bubbles attached to these outer bubbles to flesh out smaller details. So if your world were polytheistic, you'd write this trait in a bubble, and then add a few names of your universe's deities in smaller bubbles.

Once you're done, transfer your ideas over to a word-processing document, and start building your outline. If you're clear enough, just go ahead and start writing.

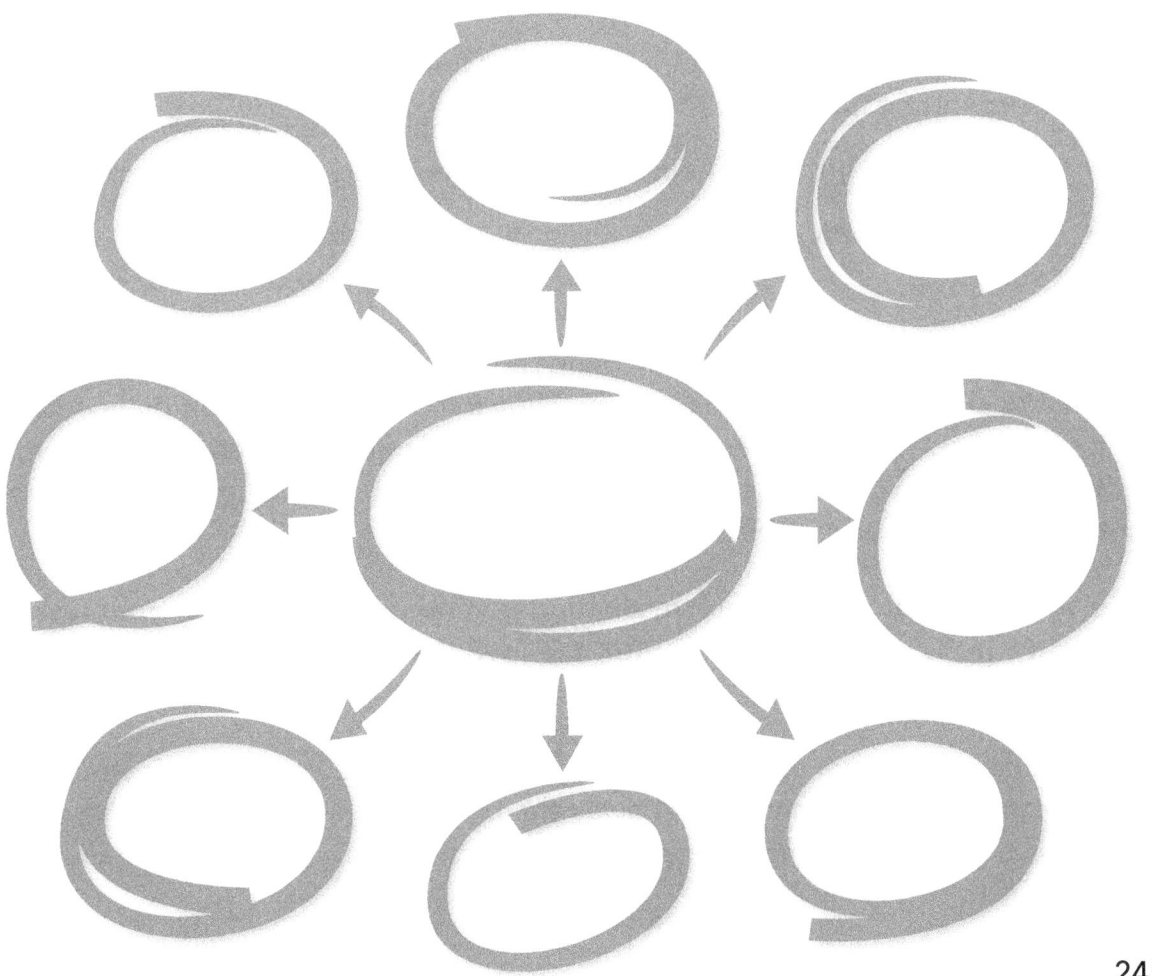

What's the Hold Up?

Does this scenario sound familiar? You think about sitting down to write, but then you find yourself:

- Lost in music videos on YouTube
- Reorganizing the closets
- Scrolling through social media
- Taking artsy photos of your cat
- Researching stock prices
- Going for a run
- Shopping for that perfect something you don't need
- Doing something else, *anything* else

You get the picture. Chances are these things aren't actually distracting you from what you want to do. Rather, you're making the choice to put off what you planned to do, and it's become a habit. In other words, you're **actively procrastinating**. Maybe you're being productive in other ways, but that's not going to work in the long run if you *really* want to produce a good piece of writing.

Once you admit you've been procrastinating getting down to writing, your task is to figure out why. Is it a fear of failure? Is it the idea that circumstances need to be just right? Is it because you don't want to write as much as you think you do?

There can be any number of factors involved in procrastination, so if this is your version of Writer's Block, you'll want to peel away the layers and figure out why the sight of your cat in a spot of sun is more deserving of your time than the process of writing.

To start getting to the bottom of this, name all the things that you do instead of writing and, most important, *why* you do them:

Go on a Writeabout

In the Aborigine culture of Australia, a walkabout is a rite of passage into adulthood. Rites of passage aside, we've all heard this term bandied about in other ways, but the gist is the same: it's a journey—maybe one with purpose or maybe none at all.

A writeabout is similar: You will be going on a foot journey through the wilds of your neighborhood—maybe you'll stop at a shopping mall, a grocery store, a park, the woods, a neighborhood hangout, and wherever else your feet take you.

1. Set aside a day for this, put on some good walking shoes, and take this book with you. You'll need it. Think of this as your "write" of passage into writerhood.

2. Don't plan your stops. Just let your feet take you there. If you live in rural area, go ahead and drive or bus to a particular destination that gives you the opportunity to simply walk around and experience life.

3. As you walkabout, notice the sights, sounds, and smells around you. Reach out and touch things (no, not that lady lugging all those shopping bags). Eat breakfast, lunch, and dinner at different spots, and pay particular attention to how the food tastes.

4. During this journey, stop every 20 minutes to take notes on what you are experiencing. Describe your sensations in such a way that a reader who isn't with you could vicariously have the same experience.

5. When the day is done, head home. Review your notes, and if you feel inspired to expand upon a particular experience or the whole day, get to it.

Field Notes:

If you need more room, use the blanks in the back.

Evening Journaling with a Twist

Some people journal every night before bed. Maybe they reflect on the day in a diary-like way or perhaps they write down a few things they appreciate in a gratitude journal. These are excellent habits for winding down the day. But even if you do one or both of these things, let's add a twist.

In the space below or in your bedside journal, write down *one* thing you want to write about tomorrow. Maybe it's a particular scene between your characters, a new section of your self-help manual, or an idea for an article.

_____
_____
_____
_____
_____
_____

What feelings do you want to convey to your reader?
_____
_____

How do you want your reader to feel after they've read that part?

Did anything that happened today bring up those feelings for you? Describe it.

Your Authentic Voice

Your writer's voice is the distinctive way you choose and arrange words and employ literary devices to convey images and ideas. The more comfortable you are with your voice, the more your words will flow. And the more you write, the more you'll establish your unique voice.

The thesaurus comes in handy when you're stumped for a word, but do you often find yourself scouring the thesaurus for a "better" way to say something? If you find yourself typing words you'd never use in real life, you may still be a little shaky with your writer's voice—and that may be the source of your current troubles.

There's nothing wrong with expanding your vocabulary. In fact, it's highly recommended. The idea, though, is to start using the words you learn in casual conversation before you incorporate them into your writing. This way, they will be authentically yours.

If you find you can't work a word comfortably into your everyday diction, it might be better to find a more organic alternative. If a word doesn't sound natural to you when you speak it, it may not sound natural when a reader reads it. So go *au natural* as much as possible in your writing to fully embrace the authentic writer in you.

What new word will use in casual conversation the next chance you get?

Make Some Social Plans

Sometimes introversion works out in a writer's favor. They'd rather be alone putting their thoughts on paper than be part of the social scene's hustle and bustle. Still, amidst all the hustle and bustle is where life happens and inspiration often comes a-callin'.

So, if you're coming up short on words, it's time to turn on your inner extrovert and make some social plans. Getting out from behind the desk and talking to nonfictional people can actually help you write. What's more, socializing can take your mind off whatever part of the writing process is bogging you down. If you're squirrelled away too long without human interaction, it might take a toll on your mental well-being.

If you still feel like kicking yourself for taking a break, change your mindset: Think of your going out as "research." People-watching can be quite enlightening if you're struggling to write characters, and visiting places with rich architecture of vibrant nature can help you write more vivid settings. If nonfictional pursuits are more your style, maybe you will attend a lecture with a friend or colleague or arrange a group outing to a place of interest.

Whatever the case, nurturing your social life can be good for you *and* your muse. Make a plan now:

Who are you going to call or text?_____

What social plan will you propose?_____

_____

_____

Gain Relevant Experience

It's been said that there's no substitute for experience, and in writing, it's often true. Readers (and editors) can often tell when an author is writing out of their depth. When you're writing nonfiction, you're drawing from your own personal and/or professional experiences and in-depth research. Hopefully, you already have the relevant experience you need for that!

But what if you're writing fiction? The old adage goes, "Write what you know," but you can't possibly have firsthand experience with *everything* your characters will do and experience. This doesn't mean you can't develop a basic understanding to make your writing feel more authentic. For example:

- Take a few karate classes or dance classes if your character is proficient in the study. Knowing how an action feels in the body, not just how it looks to an observer, can help you write more authentically.

- If you're writing a crime novel, take a criminology course or read up on famous cases.

- If your character is a musician, consider taking an introductory course on the instrument of their choice. If they read music, you may want to learn how to do so, too.

- If a major battle takes place in your book, read up on military strategy of an appropriate time period. You can study specific battles for reference.

- Does your character shoot a longbow or swing a sword? See if you can find a local reenactment group that could show you how those weapons might have been used.

- If your character runs a five-star hotel, splurge for an overnight stay at one.

- Visit the places and settings your characters will pass through or study up on them.

- If you're writing a scene at a restaurant, eat the foods your characters will likely order.

These are just a few ideas. As you can tell, there's ample opportunity to explore in real life what your characters experience on the written page. If you can't go out and do it yourself, interview people who have the experience you want to write about.

List three things you need to experience to write authentically:

1._____

_____

_____

2._____

_____

_____

3._____

_____

_____

Engage Your Senses

Nothing brings a scene to life as much as invoking the reader's five senses. Likewise, directly engaging your senses gives you firsthand experience of something that you can then write about with more confidence. Pick something, anything, to experience. A puppy perhaps? A lobster dinner? A bunch of flowers? A garden hose? Really, it can be absolutely anything.

Describe how it looks:

_____
_____
_____
_____
_____

Describe how it feels:

_____
_____
_____
_____
_____

    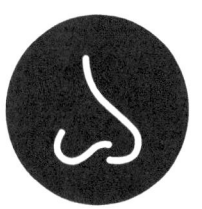

Describe how it tastes (if appropriate!):

_____
_____
_____
_____

Describe how it sounds:

_____
_____
_____
_____

Describe how it smells:

_____
_____
_____
_____

It's Got Personality

Take a look around your workspace and notice any inanimate objects you might have within reach. Choose one that's directly involved in your writing process, whether it's the pen in your hand, the computer mouse by your keyboard, or the cup you always brew your tea in when you're getting ready to write. Now it's time to personify that object—make it come alive.

Give the object a name. Choose a name that makes you smile.

_____

What's the object's favorite activity? For example, a computer mouse's favorite activity might be zipping around your desk clicking around a document or hunting for research ideas online.

_____

Does the object have a favorite snack? Maybe the pen's the one who keeps "eating" your Post-It notes!

_____

What part of the day does this object like the least? Perhaps the teacup finds its daily dishwasher ride a little scary.

_____

How does this object feel about your Writer's Block?

_____

If this object could offer you some encouragement, what would it say?

_____
_____
_____

What other personality traits would this object have? What other interests would it pursue if it could? Does it have any strong opinions on things? Fill in as many personality traits for this object as you like.

_____
_____
_____
_____
_____
_____
_____
_____
_____
_____
_____
_____

Avoiding the Spotlight?

Let's see if you can relate to this scenario: You're 99.9% ready to put your writing out into the world, and then suddenly you stop working on it. You stop. Just. Like. That.

That .01% is a looming hike up Mt. Everest. Besides, don't you have a billion other things to keep you busy? Meanwhile, you know you've put your ALL into it, and you know it's good and worthy of being shared. Others have even told you so. So really, what's stopping you from taking those final steps?

The spotlight is my guess. Not only does a bright light make you more visible to your audience, but it also makes you more visible to potential detractors. Chance are, there's always going to be someone who's jealous, who thinks they know more than you, who dislikes what you've written, who claims you don't know enough, who accuses you of being self-indulgent, or—gosh, this list could go on and on. It's suddenly like being back in the hallways of junior high.

You made it through junior high school, right? You'll make it through this, too. Don't let that small handful of people, no matter their level of expertise or influence, stop you from sharing yourself with others in whatever form your written word takes. This is you. This is yours. This is your contribution.

Focus on the people who will like what you've done and, with renewed bravery and confidence, complete that .01%. Then, when it's time to walk down the bright hallways, keep your chin high—even if someone's bullying you or whispering behind your back.

Pyramid Scheme

Maybe you're writing willy-nilly and you're not sure where your story is headed, if anywhere. Enter nineteenth-century novelist and playwright, Gustav Freytag. He created a five-part dramatic story structure that may help you find direction.

This is not the *only* story structure (there's also the three-act structure and the hero's journey structure, to name a couple), but it's a common and effective template for putting a story in order.

There are five basic parts to this story structure. Take a look.

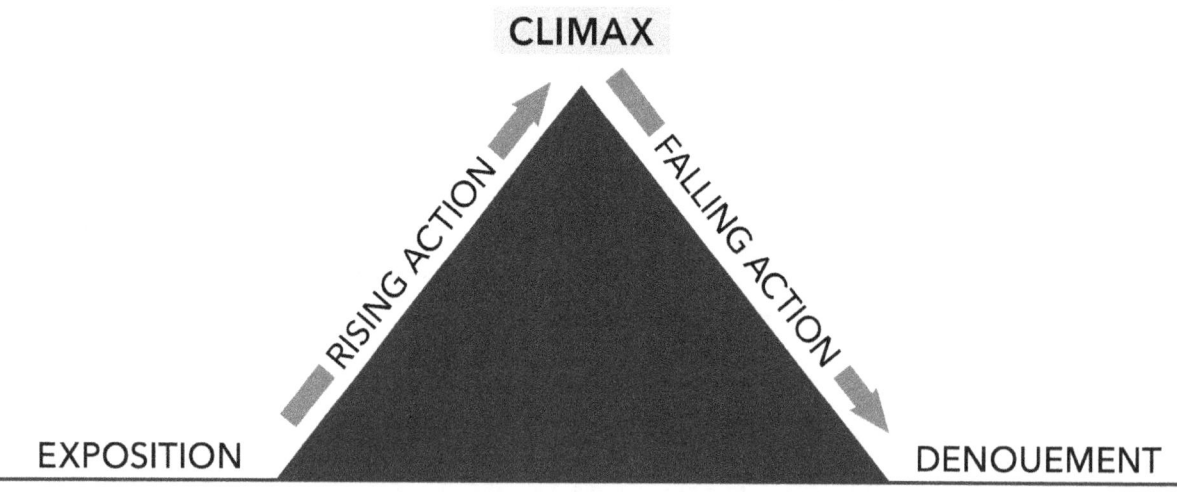

1. **Exposition** introduces the main character and sets the scene. How much and what kind of exposition is needed depends on the tone you want to set. For example, you could open in the middle of the action—with a hovercar chase over a futuristic city with your character laughing as they easily evade cyber-police. This tells the reader the time period and setting and hints at the main character's personality, all while hooking the reader into the story.

2. **Rising action** occurs after an inciting incident—the first in a chain reaction of events the main character experiences. How they react determines how the suspense and action build toward the climax. Say your character loses a close friend under mysterious circumstances. Their choice to react by investigating that loss makes the reader want to know what's really going on, and the suspense builds as the character finds path to the truth is far more winding and dangerous than they thought it would be.

3. The **climax** is the tensest point of the story. It doesn't necessarily come smack in the middle; climactic events can occur earlier or later in a story. The climax usually shows the contrast between the protagonist and antagonist. Antagonists can be a single character or a group of characters, and they don't have to be outright evil; they just need to be at odds with your protagonist. The antagonist might even be a part of the main character themselves, something in their personality they must overcome in order to succeed or save the day.

4. **Falling action** refers to the change in the protagonist and the plot that follows the climax. This doesn't mean the intensity of action needs to fall; it just means the story has shifted in a different direction as a result of the climax. Character reversal can occur as a result of the climax, too. Perhaps your protagonist, having faced off against the antagonist, has realized that the antagonist isn't really their enemy, but there's some outside force that's pitting them against each other. Now the protagonist's goal is to stop this outside force, rather than the antagonist, even if their ideals are still at odds.

5. **Denouement** is French for "the ending." The resolution of the story—where the main character solves the problem they've been grappling with for the whole story—is part of this. In Shakespeare's plays, the comedies usually ended in a wedding, while the tragedies ended in multiple deaths. Effective, eh?

Using this story structure, or another, see if you can identify these points in the piece you are writing.

> "A whole is what has a beginning and middle and end." ~Aristotle

Believe in Something Else

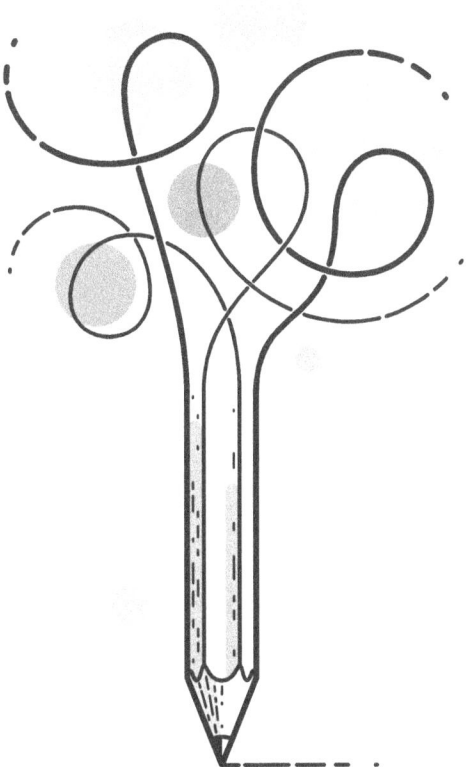

You believe in your Writer's Block, or you wouldn't be reading this. Whether it's a figment of your imagination or a concrete obstacle you need to work through, you're giving it more life by focusing on it.

Hopefully, the activities in this book have given you something else to focus on, and you're feeling more confident about moving forward with your writing project. But if you're still having trouble, it's time to believe in something else, like your abilities.

You wouldn't be a writer if it's something you're not good at it. So instead of saying, "I have Writer's Block," tell yourself, "I have strong writing abilities." Instead of saying, "I can't write a word," tell yourself, "I'm working toward renewed inspiration and motivation to express myself through the written word."

Keep telling yourself these things until you truly believe them. You owe it to yourself to own your talent, so stop "owning" your Writer's Block.

See Your Writer's Block in a New Light

Your Writer's Block is as an opportunity to stretch your imagination, expand your perspective, practice self-care, have new experiences, socialize more, and get out of your comfort zone.

When looked at this way, it can be a blessing rather than a curse, as a stepping-stone to new and improved writer's habits and ideas.

In this new light, color in the "Writer's Block" on the facing page, appreciating every facet of what it represents.

"Words! Mere words! How terrible they were! How clear, and vivid, and cruel! One could not escape from them. And yet what a subtle magic there was in them! They seemed to be able to give a plastic form to formless things, and to have a music of their own as sweet as that of viol or of lute. Mere words! Was there anything so real as words?"
~Oscar Wilde, *The Picture of Dorian Gray*

The Blanks in the Back

These blank pages are just itching for you to write on them. Do them a favor. Put some words on them. Any words, even silly ones! They won't judge. Hammer out that Writer's Block and unleash the fire of creativity.

The Handy Guide

Not sure what you need today? Scroll through this guide the old-fashioned way with your index finger to find an activity, exercise, or prompt that might help you break the block. Flip to that page and commit to the activity. You've got this!

Balance, Finding
Remember the "Basics" (page 106)
To Write or Not to Write (page 6)

Boredom & Lack of Interest
Connectivity Issues (page 188)
Ho Hum (page 63)
Write What You Love (page 201)

Brain Workouts
A Word Break (page 230)
Classical Boost (page 70)
Don't Scramble, Unscramble (page 100)
Filling in the Gaps (page 83)
Hack Your Brain (page 148)
It's a Little Puzzling (page 137)
Map Out Your Brain (page 102)
Reveal the Hidden Message (page 142)
Show Me (page 57)

Stephy's Dilemma (page 54)
Uncover the Writing Advice (page 167)

Clarity Around Your Topic/Idea
Connect the Dots for Clarity (see page 232)
Gain Relevant Experience (page 254)
Helpline (page 207)
Hey, What's the Big Idea?! (page 194)
Ideas Bubbling Up (page 244)
Say What You Gotta Write (page 238)
Short on "Newsfeed" Content? (page 210)
Start Vague (page 198)

Coloring Pages for Mental Relaxation
(Remember, markers will bleed through the pages, so used colored pencils or crayons.)
Brain Freeze (page 51)

Breathe, Write (page 153)
Busting Stress (page 159)
Plant Your Garden (page 223)
Power-Up Phrase (page 77)
See Your Writer's Block in a New Light (page 267)
Take an Elephant Break (page 47)
The Writing Spider (page 31)

Commitments, Making

Make a Pledge (page 42)
Perfect the Art of Imperfection (page 65)
Remember Your Writing "Whys" (page 15)

Details & Description

A Picture Is Worth a Thousand Words (page 114)
Bedeviled by the [Details] (page 20)
Gather Your Props (page 22)
So Many Rules, So Little Written (page 125)
What a Character! (page 220)

Distractions, Eliminating

Day Job Distractions (page 218)
Drowning in Digital Distractions (page 208)
What's the Hold Up? (page 246)

Fatigue—Mind or Body

Brain Freeze (page 50)
Breathe, Write (page 152)
Cuppa Joe (page 133)
Embrace the Sloth (page 24)
Nighty-Night (page 122)
Screening for Problems (page 131)

Fear of Stuff

Avoiding the Spotlight? (page 260)
Debunk Your Inner Critic (page 90)
Fear Factor: Rejection (page 119)
Frozen in Fear (page 139)

Feedback, Value of

A Matter of Opinion (page 154)
Debunk Your Inner Critic (page 90)
Get Another Writer's Perspective (page 101)
Helpline (page 207)
Professional Feedback (page 82)

Grammar Worries

So Many Rules, So Little Written (page 125)

Inadequacy, Feelings of

"Do I Suck at This?" (page 156)
"Impostor!" (page 175)

Leaving on a Thought Plane (page 213)
Not Feeling "Good Enough"? (page 67)

Inspiration, Finding
A Dry Well of Inspiration (page 14)
Cinematic Inspiration (page 117)
Envision This (page 26)
Genius Folder for Fodder (page 191)
Go on a Writeabout (page 248)
Good Reads (page 33)
Got Muse? (page 10)
Inspiration Is Making You Wait (page 12)
Other Authors as Inspiration (page 176)
People Watch (page 240)
Read a Book (page 43)
What Can You See? (page 45)

Journaling
A Journaling Sensation (page 116)
Evening Journaling with a Twist (page 250)

Mindfulness & Metaphors
A Momentary Reset (page 80)
Breathe, Write (page 152)
8 Tree Lessons (page 146)
Emotional Overload (page 237)

Grounding (page 236)
Hack Your Brain (page 148)
Half-Baked Ideas (page 229)
In the Write Mind (page 59)
Map Out Your Brain (page 102)
Metaphorize It! (page 94)
Plant Your Garden (page 222)
Power-Up Phrase (page 76)
Shower for Power (page 231)
Wash That Block Away (page 166)

Mood & Emotions
Chase Those Cares Away (page 78)
Classical Boost (page 70)
Emotional Overload (page 237)
Get in the Mood (page 138)
No Time to Panic (page 104)
Power-Up Phrase (page 76)
Reset the Mood (page 29)

Perfection, Struggles Around
A Matter of Opinion (page 154)
Flawless Figment (page 151)
Not Feeling "Good Enough"? (page 67)
Perfect the Art of Imperfection (page 65)

Perspective, Changing

A Room with a New View (page 234)
Adopt a New Role (page 202)
Are You Being Authentic? (page 182)
Believe in Something Else (page 265)
Cube It to Use It (page 162)
Expand Your Perspective (page 205)
Get Another Writer's Perspective (page 101)
Have an Opposite Day (page 21)
Inside-Out Perspective (page 69)
Reinvent (page 127)
See Your Writer's Block in a New Light (page 266)
Shades of Gray (page 86)

Preparation

Declutter Your Space, Declutter Your Mind (page 140)
Hack Your Brain (page 148)
In the Write Mind (page 59)
Script It (page 149)
What Needs to Happen? (page 16)
Writer's Nook (page 108)

Pressure

Cracking Under Pressure? (page 134)
Get Off Your Own Back (page 136)

Procrastination

What's the Hold Up? (page 246)

Rejection

Facing Actual Rejection (page 121)
Fear Factor: Rejection (page 119)

Relationship with Writing

"Do I Suck at This?" (page 156)
Embrace the WIP (page 212)
Hate to Love It? (page 58)
How Do I Love Thee? (page 235)
Just Wanna Have Fun? (page 174)
Let Go of the Guilt (page 239)
No Compromises (page 157)
Time Travel (page 215)
Writing a Book? (page 180)
Writing Successes & Regrets (page 186)
Your Authentic Voice (page 252)

Self-Care

(It's so important!)
Breathe, Write (page 152)
Fuel Up! (page 226)
Good Morning, Sunshine! (page 130)
Make Some Social Plans (page 253)
Nighty-Night (page 122)

Not Tonight, Words, I Have a Headache (page 168)
Plant Your Garden (page 222)
Remember the "Basics" (page 106)
Stretch (page 196)
Wash That Block Away (page 166)
Work Out Something Other Than Your Brain (page 197)

Silly Fun
(with a purpose!)
A Circuitous Route (page 177)
A Walk Around the Writer's Block (page 91)
All Boxed In (page 93)
Filling in the Gaps (page 83)
Find Your Way (page 165)
Picture This . . . (page 9)
Post a WANTED Sign (page 184)
Put on Your Thinking Cap (page 206)

Stress
Busting Stress (page 158)
Lighten Your Stress Load (page 128)

Structure (When There's Too Little)
Can You See the Finish Line? (page 227)
Can't Write It? Outline It! (page 98)
Connect the Dots for Clarity (page 232)
Cracking Under Pressure? (page 134)
Establish Your Priorities (page 199)
Just Wanna Have Fun? (page 174)
Learn to Juggle (page 242)
No Compromises (page 157)
Orient Your GPS (page 161)
Pyramid Scheme (page 262)
Set a Target (page 38)
10 Short Steps to Your Short Story (page 85)
Time Yourself (page 112)
Your Weekly Planner (page 74)
Your Writing To-Do List (page 35)

Structure (When There's Too Much)
Have an Opposite Day (page 21)
Move the Finish Line (if you can) (page 228)
Move the Target (page 41)
Skip Around (page 172)
Word Count Bull's-Eye (page 169)

Word Games for Stimulation
Alphabet Ransom (page 48)
Don't Scramble, Unscramble (page 100)

Filling in the Gaps (page 83)
In Search of Words (page 36)
It's a Little Puzzling (page 137)
Reveal the Hidden Message (page 142)
Uncover the Writing Advice (page 167)
Who Wrote It? (page 178)

Writing Environment

Declutter Your Space, Declutter Your Mind (page 140)
Decorate Your Writing Space (page 150)
No Compromises (page 157)
Writer's Nook (page 108)

Writing Prompts to Get the Juices Flowing

After the Introductions . . . (page 61)
Engage Your Senses (page 256)
Falling Down the Rabbit Hole (page 111)
How to . . . (page 214)
Imagine That . . . (page 8)
Inside-Out Perspective (page 69)
It was the best of words. It was the worst of words. (page 62)
It's Got Personality (page 258)
Power Lines (page 216)
Revisit the Past (page 52)
Script It (page 149)
Show Me (page 57)
Still Life (page 97)
The Naughty List (page 144)
Then What Happened? (page 92)
30-Day Lifetime Challenge (page 224)
20 Get-Writing Prompts (page 72)
What a Character! (page 220)
What Comes to Mind? (page 192)
Write a "Bad" Page (page 170)
Write Just for Fun (page 18)
Write Short (page 187)

The Solutions

In Search of Words (page 36)

* Always the editor. The actual quote is: *"I was working on the proof of one of my poems all the morning, and took out a comma. In the afternoon I put it back again."*

**Marx actually said: *"Outside of a dog, a book is man's best friend because inside of a dog is too dark to read."* But the basic joke didn't originate with him.

Stephy's Dilemma (page 54)

Carol, Self-motivation, 1 month
Gary, Business, 4 months
Sarah, Fantasy, 3 months
Michael, Espionage, 2 months

Don't Scramble, Unscramble (page 100)

"I was working on the proof of one of my poems all the morning, and I took out a comma. In the afternoon, I put it back again." ~Oscar Wilde*

It's a Little Puzzling (page 137)

"Outside of a dog, a book is a man's best friend; inside of a dog, it's too dark to read." ~Groucho Marx**

Reveal the Hidden Message (page 142)

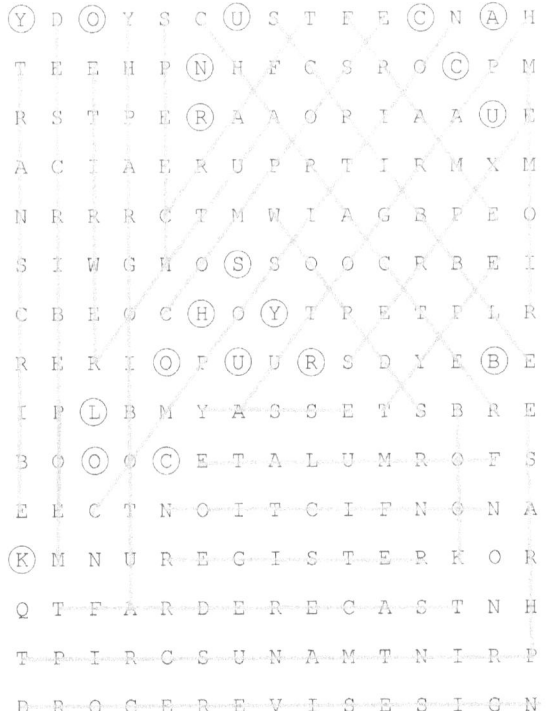

YOU CAN CRUSH YOUR BLOCK NOW

Find Your Way (page 165)

Uncover the Writing Advice (page 167)

ANSWER: "There is no rule on how to write. Sometimes it comes easily and perfectly; sometimes it's like drilling rock and then blasting it out with charges."
~Ernest Hemingway

A Circuitous Route (page 177)

A Word Break (page 230)

1	6	4	7	2	5	9	3	8
7	5	8	3	9	4	1	6	2
3	9	2	8	1	6	5	4	7
9	4	1	5	3	7	8	2	6
2	7	6	9	8	1	3	5	4
5	8	3	6	4	2	7	9	1
4	2	7	1	5	9	6	8	3
6	3	5	2	7	8	4	1	9
8	1	9	4	6	3	2	7	5

Who Wrote It? (page 178)

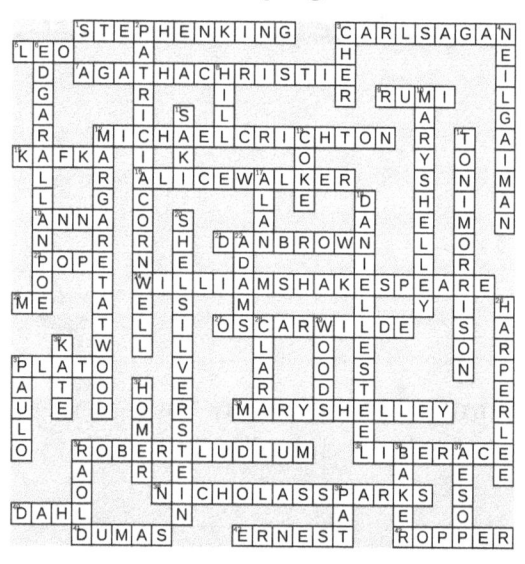

Connect These Dots (page 233)

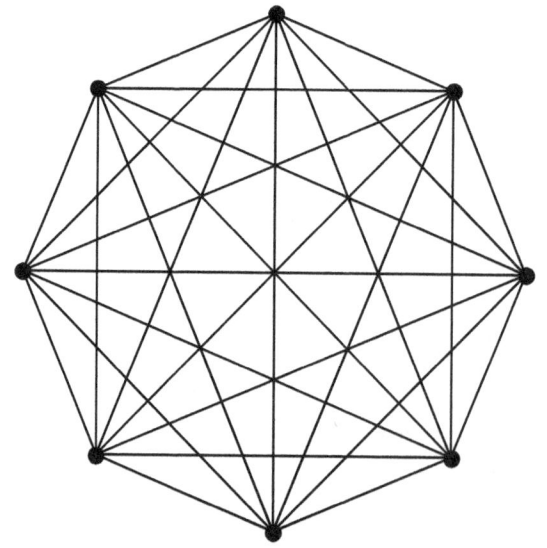

298

Quotation Sources

In order of appearance.

Jack Kerouac, unnumbered page, https://en.wikiquote.org/wiki/Jack_Kerouac and https://quotepark.com/quotes/937784-jack-kerouac-soon-ill-find-the-right-words-theyll-be-very-si/, accessed October 10, 2022.

Louis L'Amour, page 3: https://www.goodreads.com/quotes/303969-start-writing-no-matter-what-the-water-does-not-flow, accessed October 10, 2022.

Harriet Beecher Stowe, page 7, https://www.goodreads.com/quotes/64772-never-give-up-for-that-is-just-the-place-and, accessed October 10, 2022.

Charles Bukowski, page 9, https://www.goodreads.com/quotes/372045-writing-about-a-writer-s-block-is-better-than-not-writingm accessed October 10, 2022.

Barbara Kingsolver, page 11, https://www.goodreads.com/quotes/348998-i-learned-to-produce-whether-i-wanted-to-or-not, accessed October 10, 2022.

Jack London, page 13, https://quoteinvestigator.com/2011/09/21/inspiration-club/, accessed October 10, 2022.

John Rogers, page 19, https://www.goodreads.com/quotes/1305134-you-can-t-think-yourself-out-of-a-writing-block-you, accessed October 10, 2022.

Neil Gaiman, page 20, https://thepublishingculture.wordpress.com/2015/03/12/neil-gaiman-maintaining-discipline-in-your-writing/, accessed October 10, 2022.

Mark Twain (or maybe not), page 34, https://quoteinvestigator.com/2018/02/03/start/#f+17869+1+7, accessed October 10, 2022.

Confucius, page 40, https://www.readsmarty.com/2018/02/confucius-quotes.html, accessed October 10, 2022.

Lisa See, page 43, https://www.goodreads.com/quotes/469343-read-a-thousand-books-and-your-words-will-flow-like, accessed October 10, 2022.

Molière, page 46, https://www.goodreads.com/quotes/188304-the-greater-the-obstacle-the-more-glory-in-overcoming-it, accessed October 10, 2022.

Octavia E. Butler, page 52, https://www.locusmag.com/2000/Issues/06/Butler.html, accessed October 10, 2022.

Anton Chekhov, page 56, https://quoteinvestigator.com/2013/07/30/moon-glint/, accessed October 10, 2022.

Robert A. Heinlein, page 58, https://www.goodreads.com/quotes/14320-writing-is-not-necessarily-something-to-be-ashamed-of-but, accessed October 10, 2022.

Agatha Christie, page 60, https://www.gradesaver.com/and-then-there-were-none/study-guide/quotes, accessed October 10, 2022.

Margaret Atwood, page 64, https://kidadl.com/quotes/ultimate-margaret-atwood-quotes-from-the-famous-canadian-writer, accessed October 10, 2022.

Ludwig van Beethoven, 71, https://www.goodreads.com/quotes/191117-i-would-rather-write-10-000-notes-than-a-single-letter, accessed October 10, 2022.

Arthur Plotnik, page 82, https://www.goodreads.com/author/quotes/21668.Arthur_Plotnik, accessed October 10, 2022.

Aldous Huxley, page 88, https://www.goodreads.com/quotes/50163-there-are-things-known-and-there-are-things-unknown-and, accessed October 10, 2022.

Virginia Woolf, page 94, https://www.goodreads.com/quotes/23162-books-are-the-mirrors-of-the-soul, accessed October 10, 2022.

Octavius, Night at the Museum, page 95, https://www.imdb.com/title/tt0477347/characters/nm0001774, accessed October 10, 2022.

Oscar Wilde, page 116, https://www.goodreads.com/quotes/8079-i-never-travel-without-my-diary-one-should-always-have, accessed October 10, 2022.

Saul Bellow, page 118, https://www.theguardian.com/books/2005/apr/06/saulbellow, accessed October 10, 2022.

John Lydgate, page 120, https://www.goodreads.com/quotes/699462-you-can-please-some-of-the-people-all-of-the, accessed October 10, 2022.

John Steinbeck, page 123, https://www.goodreads.com/quotes/990924-it-is-a-common-experience-that-a-problem-difficult-at, accessed October 10, 2022.

Pablo Picasso, page 124, https://www.goodreads.com/quotes/558213-learn-the-rules-like-a-pro-so-you-can-break, accessed October 10, 2022.

Orson Scott Card, page 126, https://www.writerswrite.com/journal/orson-scott-card-9992, accessed October 10, 2022.

David Allen, page 129, https://www.goodreads.com/quotes/242674-you-can-do-anything-but-not-everything, accessed October 10, 2022.

Gary Larson, The Far Side, page 132, https://www.goodreads.com/quotes/672757-i-don-t-know-where-my-ideas-come-from-i-will, accessed October 10, 2022.

Joss Whedon, page 138, https://www.goodreads.com/quotes/150924-write-it-shoot-it-publish-it-crochet-it-saut-it, accessed October 10, 2022.

Babe Ruth, page 139, https://www.goodreads.com/quotes/916753-don-t-let-the-fear-of-striking-out-hold-you-back, accessed October 10, 2022.

Oscar Wilde, page 145, https://www.goodreads.com/quotes/208595-a-writer-is-someone-who-has-taught-his-mind-to, accessed October 10, 2022.

Salvador Dalí, page 151, https://www.goodreads.com/quotes/18874-have-no-fear-of-perfection---you-ll-never-reach-it, accessed October 10, 2022.

Pat Pattison, page 156, https://www.goodreads.com/quotes/921590-i-hereby-grant-you-permission-to-write-crap-the-more, accessed October 10, 2022.

Vincent Van Gogh, page 160, https://www.goodreads.com/quotes/75899-great-things-are-not-done-by-impulse-but-by-a, accessed October 10, 2022.

J.R.R. Tolkien, *The Fellowship of the Ring*, page 164, https://www.goodreads.com/quotes/229-all-that-is-gold-does-not-glitter-not-all-those, accessed October 10, 2022.

Dr. Seuss, page 169, https://www.goodreads.com/quotes/176857-so-the-writer-who-breeds-more-words-than-he-needs?page=4, accessed October 10, 2022.

Jodi Picoult, page 171, https://www.goodreads.com/quotes/568141-you-can-always-edit-a-bad-page-you-can-t-edit, accessed October 10, 2022.

Jean-Luc Godard, page 173, https://www.goodreads.com/quotes/276063-a-story-should-have-a-beginning-a-middle-and-an, accessed October 10, 2022.

William S. Burroughs, page 183, https://www.goodreads.com/quotes/330803-cheat-your-landlord-if-you-can-and-must-but-do, accessed October 10, 2022.

Richard Bach, page 186, https://www.goodreads.com/quotes/25672-a-professional-writer-is-an-amateur-who-didn-t-quit, accessed October 10, 2022.

Albert Einstein, Page 191, https://www.goodreads.com/quotes/38836-imagination-is-everything-it-is-the-preview-of-life-s-coming, accessed October 10, 2022.

Natalie Goldberg, page 200, https://www.goodreads.com/quotes/109425-trust-in-what-you-love-continue-to-do-it-and, accessed October 10, 2022.

Willy Wonka, page 206, https://quoteinvestigator.com/2016/09/27/nonsense/, accessed October 10, 2022.

William H. Gass, page 214, https://www.goodreads.com/quotes/188928-the-true-alchemists-do-not-change-lead-into-gold-they, accessed October 10, 2022.

C. S. Lewis, page 221, https://www.goodreads.com/quotes/16986-you-can-make-anything-by-writing, accessed October 10, 2022.

Aristotle, page 264, http://www.perseus.tufts.edu/hopper/text?doc=Aristot.+Poet.+1450b&redirect=true, accessed October 10, 2022.

Oscar Wilde, *The Picture of Dorian Gray*, page 268, https://www.goodreads.com/quotes/11777-words-mere-words-how-terrible-they-were-how-clear-and, accessed October 10, 2022.

SOLUTIONS

Ernest Hemingway, page 167, https://www.goodreads.com/quotes/27293-there-is-no-rule-on-how-to-write-sometimes-it, accessed October 10, 2022.

Oscar Wilde, page 100, https://www.goodreads.com/quotes/314-i-was-working-on-the-proof-of-one-of-my, accessed October 10, 2022.

Groucho Marx, page 137, https://quoteinvestigator.com/2010/09/08/dog/, accessed October 10, 2022.

Activity/Exercise Index

A
Adopt a New Role, 202–203
After the Introductions . . . , 61
All Boxed In, 93
Alphabet Ransom, 48–49
Are You Being Authentic?, 182–183
Avoiding the Spotlight?, 260–261

B
Bedeviled by the [Details], 20
Believe in Something Else, 265
Brain Freeze, 50
Brain Freeze, coloring page, 51
Breathe, Write, 152
Breathe, Write, coloring page, 153
Busting Stress, 158
Busting Stress, coloring page, 159

C
Can You See the Finish Line?, 227
Can't Write It? Outline It!, 98–99
Chase Those Cares Away, 78–79
Cinematic Inspiration, 117
Circuitous Route, A, 177
Classical Boost, 70–71
Connect the Dots for Clarity, 232
Connect These Dots, 233
Connectivity Issues, 188–189
Cracking Under Pressure, 134–135
Cube It to Use It, 162–163
Cuppa Joe, 133

D
Day Job Distractions, 218–219
Debunk Your Inner Critic, 90
Declutter Your Space, Declutter Your Mind, 140–141
Decorate Your Writing Space, 150
"Do I Suck at This?", 156
Don't Scramble, Unscramble, 100
Drowning in Digital Distractions, 208–209
Dry Well of Inspiration, A, 14

E
8 Tree Lessons, 146
8 Tree Lessons, coloring page, 147
Embrace the Sloth, 24–25
Embrace the WIP, 212
Emotional Overload, 237
Engage Your Senses, 256–257
Envision This, 26–27
Establish Your Priorities, 199
Evening Journaling with a Twist, 250–251
Expand Your Perspective, 205

F
Facing Actual Rejection, 121
Falling Down the Rabbit Hole, 111
Fear Factor: Rejection, 119
Filling in the Gaps, 83–84
Find Your Way, 165
Flawless Figment, 151
Frozen in Fear, 139
Fuel Up!, 226

G
Gain Relevant Experience, 254–255
Gather Your Props, 22–23
Genius Folder for Fodder, 191
Get Another Writer's Perspective, 101
Get in the Mood, 138
Get Off Your Own Back, 136
Go on a Writeabout, 248–249
Good Morning, Sunshine!, 130
Good Reads, 33
Got Muse?, 10
Grounding, 236

H
Hack Your Brain, 148
Half-Baked Ideas, 229
Hate to Love It?, 58
Have an Opposite Day, 21
Helpline, 207
Hey, What's the Big Idea?!, 194–195
Ho Hum, 63
How Do I Love Thee?, 235
How to . . . , 214

I
Ideas Bubbling Up, 244–245
Imagine That . . . , 8
"Impostor!", 175
In Search of Words, 36–37
In the Write Mind, 59
Inside-Out Perspective, 69
Inspiration Is Making You Wait, 12–13
It was the best of words. It was the worst of words., 62
It's a Little Puzzling, 137
It's Got Personality, 258–259

J
Journaling Sensation, A, 116
Just Wanna Have Fun?, 174

L
Learn to Juggle, 242–243
Leaving on a Thought Plane, 213
Let Go of the Guilt, 239
Lighten Your Stress Load, 128–129

M
Make a Pledge, 42
Make Some Social Plans, 253
Map Out Your Brain, 102–103
Matter of Opinion, A, 154–155
Metaphorize It!, 94–95
Momentary Reset, A, 80–81
Move the Finish Line (if you can), 228
Move the Target, 41

N
Nighty-Night, 122–123
No Compromises, 157
No Time to Panic, 104–105
Not Feeling "Good Enough"?, 67
Not Tonight, MS Word, I Have a Headache, 168

O
Orient Your GPS, 161
Other Authors as Inspiration, 176

P
People Watch, 240–241
Perfect the Art of Imperfection, 65
Picture Is Worth a Thousand Words, A, 114–115
Picture This . . . , 9
Plant Your Garden, 222
Plant Your Garden, coloring page, 223
Post a WANTED Sign, 184–185
Power Lines, 216–217
Power-Up Phrase, 76
Power-Up Phrase, coloring page, 77
Professional Feedback, 82
Put on Your Thinking Cap, 206
Pyramid Scheme, 262–264

R
Read a Book, 43
Reinvent, 127
Remember the "Basics", 106–107
Remember Your Writing "Whys", 15
Reset the Mood, 29
Reveal the Hidden Message, 142–143
Revisit the Past, 52–53
Room with a New View, A, 234

S
Say What You Gotta Write, 238
Screening for Problems, 131
Script It, 149
See Your Writer's Block in a New Light, 266
See Your Writer's Block in a New Light, coloring page, 267
Set a Target, 38–39
Shades of Gray, 86–87
Short on "Newsfeed" Content, 210–211
Show Me, 57
Shower for Power, 231
Skip Around, 172–173
So Many Rules, So Little Written, 125
Start Vague, 198
Stephy's Dilemma, 54–55
Still Life, 97
Stretch, 196

T
Take an Elephant Break, 46
Take an Elephant Break, coloring page, 47
10 Short Steps to Your Short Story, 85
The Naughty List, 144–145
The Writing Spider, 30
The Writing Spider, coloring page, 31
Then What Happened?, 92
30-Day Lifetime Challenge, 224–225
Time Travel, 215
Time Yourself, 112–113
To Write or Not to Write, 6
20 Get-Writing Prompts, 72–73

U
Uncover the Writing Advice, 167

W
Walk Around the Writer's Block, A, 91
Wash That Block Away, 166
What a Character!, 220–221
What Can You See?, 45
What Comes to Mind?, 192–193
What Needs to Happen?, 16–17
What's the Hold Up?, 246–247
Who Wrote It?, 178–179
Word Break, A, 230
Word Count Bull's-Eye, 169
Work Out Something Other Than Your Brain, 197
Write a "Bad" Page, 170–171
Write Just for Fun, 18–19
Write Short, 187
Write What You Love, 201
Writer's Nook, 108–109
Writing a Book?, 180–181
Writing Successes & Regrets, 186

Y
Your Authentic Voice, 252
Your Weekly Planner, 74–75
Your Writing To-Do List, 35

Thanks!

Thank you to the many awesome authors I've had the pleasure of guiding through the writing and editing process over the last twenty-plus years. I never tire of witnessing the birth of a new book or other creative idea. Let's keep 'em coming!

Thank you to Gary Rosenberg, not only for being such a giving, considerate, and loving husband but also for being a dependable, tireless, and talented business partner. But even more than that, thank you for entertaining my per-fectionism on every project we work on together, including this one (grumbles not withstanding). You are the back cover to my front cover—sort of like the wind beneath my wings.

Thank you to my editor, Sarah Winklbauer, for her insight, creativity, and support. You are treasured for your skills, authentic goofiness, and friendship. I couldn't have completed this book without you.

Thank you to Rudy Shur and all my former colleagues at Avery Publishing, Square One Publishers, and Penguin-Putnam. It is because of you that I am where I am, professionally speaking. Your lessons went a long way. Fortunately, I have a good memory.

Thank you to Justin Rosenberg, who is always quick with unique, witty, and creative ideas as well as thought-provoking insight. Thank you to Michael Castellanos, who brainstormed ideas with me for this book before it was even a manuscript. Thank you to Rachel Arvelo, too, just for being you. Thank you, Stephanie Castellanos, for being a bright addition to our lives. I love you all.

Thanks to all my friends. I appreciate your support and belief in me. Special thanks to my long-time publishing colleagues turned priceless friends: Michele Matrisciani, Kim Weiss, and Lisa McCourt. Your friendship, love, and professional support are invaluable. Special thanks to Deborah Shapiro for always being a loving, listening ear and for reminding me to sit correctly in my office chair. More special thanks to Dawn Maslar-Biggie for her friendship and examples of dreaming big. And to the remaining Royal, Jennifer Thornton, for her contagious enthusiasm. And even more special thanks to my lifelong companions and dear friends: Annamaria Boice, Antonietta Tarnell, and Donna Diblasio. You've certainly been filling my life bucket with fun and interesting adventures. And to my Spuds—Dara Stewart, Phaedra Mastrocola, and Justine Poldino—thank you for all the laughter and also the heartfelt tears. To LeeAnn Angelone and Amber Page, not only are you my friends but you're also my family, and I couldn't imagine life without your unwavering support. And to Joely Leidner, of course—thanks for the decades of friendship. To all my friends not mentioned by name, I appreciate having you in my life. Thank you, everyone. I love all of you.

To my brothers and sisters—thank you all for giving me the unique perspective of being the youngest. Maryanne, special thanks for listening to my ideas and cheering me on. To my cousins and cousins-in-law, my in-laws, and my nieces and nephews and their growing families—you each offer your love freely and add a colorful dimension to my life. I love you, each and every one.

To my mother-in-law, Gloria Rosenberg, and my father-in-law, Henry Rosenberg. You have both made so many of our dreams possible. Your love and support are cherished, today and always.

To my parents, James and Theresa Killman. Daddy, thanks for all the entertaining stories and for giving me that essential creative spark. Mommy, thank you for being the foundation upon which the rest of my life was built and for instilling in me the love of home.

Thanks to Chiku, Urielle, Rook, and Majesty for keeping me from sitting at my desk for overly long stretches. You brighten my day.

Thanks, everybody!

About the Author

CAROL KILLMAN ROSENBERG is a seasoned editor and book coach, specializing in developmental editing, substantive editing, and creative editing, with twenty-four years of experience in the traditional book publishing industry. She currently resides in Boca Raton, Florida, with her husband, Gary, and their animal companions, Chiku, Urielle, Rook, and Majesty.

To learn more, visit www.CarolKillmanRosenberg.com and www.TheBookCouple.com.

www.ingramcontent.com/pod-product-compliance
Lightning Source LLC
Chambersburg PA
CBHW082221090526
44585CB00020BA/2207